CHOOSING

A New Way to Respond

Other Books by Edward E. Ford

Why Marriage?
Coauthored with Robert L. Zorn
Why Be Lonely?

Coauthored with Steven L. Englund
For the Love of Children
Permanent Love

Contributed chapters to:
What Are You Doing?: How People Are Helped Through Reality Therapy
Family Counseling and Therapy

CHOOSING TO LOVE

A New Way to Respond

Edward E. Ford

WINSTON PRESS

Cover design: Studio One

ISBN (paperback): 0-86683-695-0

ISBN (hardcover): 0-86683-749-3

Library of Congress Catalog Card Number: 82-51156

Printed in the United States of America.

5 4 3 2 1

Winston Press, Inc.
430 Oak Grove
Minneapolis, Minnesota 55403

For Hester

Everyone thinks of changing the world, but no one thinks of changing himself.

—Leo Tolstoy

Contents

Acknowledgments

Many of the thoughts and ideas in this book can be traced directly to a theory called "Behavior: The Control of Perception," or BCP psychology. This was first set forth by William Powers in his book by that title (Aldine Press, 1973). It was further developed and made practical by William Glasser, M.D., in his book, *Stations Of The Mind* (Harper & Row, 1981). I am indebted to Dr. Glasser for teaching me BCP psychology.

I am indebted to Steven Englund and Robert L. Zorn, who coauthored earlier books with me. Steven, who worked with me on *Permanent Love* (Winston Press, 1979) and *For The Love Of Children* (Anchor Press/Doubleday, 1977), has always had confidence in my ability to think and respect for the thoughts I expressed, especially during a very critical period in my life. Bob, who helped me write *Why Marriage?* (Argus Communications, 1974) and *Why Be Lonely?* (Argus Communications, 1975), taught me the pleasure of writing. I am grateful to Father Joseph Lucas, professor, Youngstown State University, for teaching me the joy of learning. I am indebted to Robert E. Bulkley, Gary Applegate, Robert E. Wubbolding, Ann Lutter, Michael J. Murphy, and Mary Ann Wall, who have helped me along the way.

And I am most appreciative to Jim Soldani, with whom I have spent many long hours of discussion. We have worked together to tie BCP psychology to the world of business and to understand the problems of relationships more clearly. Win Smith, Executive Vice-President and General Manager of Smitty's Super Valu, Inc., has given me valuable support. So has Harry Hollack, Director of Components Production, Intel Corporation. I am grateful to them both.

Attorney Frederick J. Shaw, M.S.W., J.D., a certified reality therapist, has offered many helpful suggestions, as have the delightful, curious, and questioning people who have been taking my classes at the Franciscan Renewal Center in Scottsdale, Arizona. I am especially grateful to Miriam Frost, Managing Editor, Trade Department, Winston Press, for her continued support and encouragement from the very beginning; to my editor, Pamela Espeland, whose efforts on my behalf are deeply appreciated; to Pat Lassonde, copy editor; and a big thanks to my talented and patient secretary, Frances Rehm.

Finally, I want to thank Hester, for being her wonderful self, and all our children: Dorothy, Terry, John, Nelson, Mary Ellen, Joseph, Thomas, and Luke. Each, in his or her own way, has helped me to understand what loving is all about.

Edward E. Ford

Scottsdale, Arizona
Nov. 18, 1982

1

Figuring out what to do with what you want once you have it

Mary was an attractive twenty-six-year-old marketing representative with an electronics firm. She had been married to Bill, a thirty-one-year-old attorney, for four years. Recently Mary had begun an affair with Bill's best friend, Jim. Her reason: She was finding Bill "rather boring" these days. Her dilemma: Should she file for divorce, or not?

"I guess I'm a little confused," she told me, "and I just don't know what to do. It's not that Bill is a bad person; it's just that there doesn't seem to be anything there anymore. And besides," she added, "I'm getting to the age when I'll have to decide whether I want children."

"How do you see me helping you?" I asked.

"I guess I want you to tell me what to do."

"Do you want me to take responsibility for what you should do?" I prodded.

"I guess not," she admitted.

"I can help you take a look at what you want and what you're doing so that you can more clearly evaluate your alternatives," I went on. "I can help you to make a plan of action. Perhaps I can teach you some things that may enable you to work out your problem for yourself."

Mary looked at me thoughtfully for a moment. Then she said, "What you could teach me is how to be happy with another person. That's what I really want. I'm not happy with Bill, and I'm not too proud of my relationship with Jim." She paused before adding, "Good Lord, it seems that no one gets along with anyone for very long these days. *Doesn't anyone know how to love?"*

* * *

Mark was a thirty-one-year-old policeman who had been on the force for eight years. He claimed to be satisfied with his job and described it as "something he had always wanted to do." Yet, he confessed, "My life is empty, and I don't know what is wrong."

He and his wife, Kathy, had been married for seven years and had two children—a boy, six, and a girl, three. Kathy, twenty-eight years old, worked part-time in a day care center and attended the local community college.

"I'm nervous and upset all the time," Mark told me. "Maybe it's my nerves. My doctor says I'm under too much stress and wants to give me pills. I don't need pills! I shouldn't have to take them. I just don't know what's wrong. I yell at my wife. I scream at my kids. On my job, I'm spending most of my time handling domestic fights—more of the same. Crazy, isn't it?"

He looked down at his hands. "Maybe Kathy and I shouldn't have gotten married. Maybe we shouldn't have had kids." His eyes met mine again. "You know, my first marriage ended in six months. I was too young then. But I'm over thirty now, and I should be able to get along with a woman.

"Don't get me wrong," he said hurriedly. "I love Kathy. Maybe it's not her. Maybe I'm the one who's screwed up. Hell, I don't know *what's* wrong!"

* * *

Both Mary and Mark had *wanted* to be married. And they had *wanted* to be married to specific individuals—Bill and Kathy. Mark had *wanted* more, so he and his wife had had two children. Now he and Kathy had a family of their own—something they had *wanted* together.

But neither Mary nor Mark was happy. Mary had started an affair with Jim in an attempt to find happiness and had come up empty. Mark had gone to his doctor in an attempt to find some answers and had been advised to take pills.

Jim wasn't the cure Mary needed. Pills weren't the cure Mark needed. Each had approached me in the hope that they would find the answer through therapy.

There was one conclusion I could draw about both of them at the outset, and that proved to be our starting point: *Mary and Mark had gotten what they wanted but still were not satisfied.*

That's because the problem is not just one of getting what you want. *It's figuring out what to do with what you want once you have it.* Mary and Mark had both married— something they wanted—and ended up back at square one, more frustrated than ever. They discovered that what they *thought* would make them happy couldn't after all.

A psychological theory called "Behavior: The Control of Perception," or BCP psychology, can help us to understand this paradox, this discrepancy between what happens when we want something and what happens when we finally get it. This theory teaches that built into our brains are fixed *needs*. These needs are what motivate us. We also have an internal world of *wants*— specific things through which we believe our needs can be met. These wants vary from person to person. Finally, we have a *perceptual system* which takes in the external world and translates it in such a way that we can deal with that world. We then venture into it in an attempt to fulfill our wants and, through them, our needs.

Like wants, perceptions vary from person to person. But there is a characteristic we all have in common: When what we want and what we perceive are the same, we are satisfied. Conversely, when what we want and what we perceive are *not* the same, we are *not* satisfied. The difference between what we want to perceive and what we perceive creates within our brain a *perceptual error,* or difference, or, to put it more simply, pure pain or stress. And this pain or stress drives our *behavioral system* to try to resolve the difference between what we want and what we perceive and bring them into harmony.

Since we are born with very few natural behaviors, however, we must *learn what to do* to rectify this difference. Luckily, our behavioral system is flexible and capable of changing. We can decide which behaviors are helpful and which are not and develop a plan to alter our behavior. In short, we are responsible for what we do. Through our behaviors, we can change our perceptions of the way things are to the way we want them to be and, in the process, reduce stress and meet our needs. In other words, *behavior is the control of perception.*

When I first heard about these ideas, I questioned them. How could we change our perceptions? Weren't they real? Didn't they tell us how things actually were? And, if so, wouldn't altering our perceptions lead to self-deception? The more I thought about these ideas, though, the more the pieces fell into place. And the more I used them with the people who came to see me, the more effective I became in my work and my life.

I know, for example, that it's not enough to find persons to build our lives with. We must also learn how to behave with these persons to make living with them a satisfying experience.

There seems to be something inside each of us that makes us feel satisfied or unsatisfied with how our lives are going. That something—which sets us apart from the objects around us—is the fact that we're driven by needs.

In contrast, the typewriter I'm using to write this book has no needs whatsoever. It doesn't care whether I use it or not. It doesn't care whether I turn it on or leave it off. It just rests on my desk, and it will keep on doing that until someone moves it or the desk collapses. Meanwhile, it's indifferent to being covered or uncovered, cleaned or not cleaned. It's indifferent to the room temperature and the surrounding decor.

This very simple illustration can be used to make a point: The typewriter doesn't *want* anything because there is nothing in it—no *need*—that demands satisfaction through a want. We humans, on the other hand, have many needs and we want lots of things. We want money, friends, food, and drink; we want to enjoy sex (most of us do, at least); we want a place to live, a place to rest; we want to have fun, to know about things and people; we're eternally curious about places. Understanding what makes us want things is important. The key to helping Mary and Mark was in helping them to understand why getting what we want isn't sufficient.

Mary had a good job, a husband, and a lover. Mark had a job he professed to like, a wife, and children. Both had gotten what they wanted and initially had been satisfied. But neither had learned *how to stay in love*— how to maintain a love-need satisfaction with their partners. Neither had learned that remaining close to others takes conscious work and effort.

Your human need for love isn't satisfied automatically when the person you want makes a commitment to you. Maintaining any relationship, especially a marriage, requires a great deal of planning and patience. Couples don't "fall out of love" (they don't "fall in love," either, but that's another matter). Instead, they simply stop working on their relationships. They stop giving their relationships the care and attention and supervision necessary to keep them viable and strong. And when conflicts arise, these relationships disintegrate.

I suspect that relationships that come apart at the seams do so because they never really satisfied the partners' need for love. For when that need *is* satisfied, couples can usually handle the large and small problems they face each day. When you get something you want, and you have figured out what to do with that something to satisfy a need, you tend to put more energy into keeping it.

It is critical to understand the difference between wants and needs. Wants are very flexible and specific. They can change from moment to moment, depending on our priorities and surrounding circumstances. Needs, however, are not flexible. They do not change. They motivate our actions throughout the whole of our lives.

I have the human need for *love*. My wife, Hester, is the person—the specific want—through whom I choose to fulfill this love-need. I also choose to fulfill this need through my children. I have the basic need for *food*. I may satisfy that need through a variety of wants. I may choose an apple or a baked potato, a salad or a vegetable dish. The specific wants to fulfill our needs, human and basic, can vary from person to person.

There are other basic needs that we are continually trying to satisfy. Our brains are always checking the *water* supply in our bodies, alerting us to the need through the feeling of thirst. When we feel tired, we are experiencing the basic need for *rest*. The basic needs for water, rest, and food must be met if our bodies are to keep functioning. Satisfying another need—the basic need for *sex*—is not necessary to our survival, but it is certainly a driving force for most of us. I define sex as a basic need because it is the means we have been given to keep our species going. It can also be, as we shall see later, a want and an illusion.

We have the human need to control, which means the ability to affect the world around us, including at times, the people around us. This need for *control* ties in closely to what we do, what we want, how we go about getting what we want, and how we live our lives. It synchronizes our wants with our perceptions and behaviors. One of the greatest deterrents to marriage today is the false belief that marriage somehow means relinquishing control of our lives: I am convinced that this belief is the main reason why so many couples live together without being married. Yet, in a close and loving marriage, *no control exists*. The more one partner attempts to control the other, the less secure a marriage becomes, and the less the love-need is satisfied.

Another human need is that for *enjoyment* or *fun*. Too many adults seem to have forgotten all about this need. And when it does emerge, they don't know how to go about satisfying it. The key to fun is *effort*. Fun isn't passive; it's active. (Can any of us really claim that watching TV is "fun"?) Fun requires initiative and the willingness to expend energy. In my work, I have found that fun in the form of play activity can help couples to reach new heights of love. I once suggested to a couple to begin playing hide-and-seek with each other on a daily basis. They were skeptical at first—and then their relationship rapidly began to strengthen. From this they were able to build strength back into their marriage.

We also have the human need for *dignity* and *self-worth*, the need to be valued as human beings for what we do and who we are. Animals don't have this need. When a greyhound finishes a race, it couldn't care less which dog won. When a beaver finishes a dam, it has no sense of accomplishment. This is because animal behaviors are instinctive rather than chosen, programmed rather than creative. A bird that belongs to a species of round-nest builders will never deviate from this pattern by building a square nest or one with a patio. Individuality is the hallmark of human behavior, the characteristic that leads to our sense of self-worth.

The need to *belong* is another important human need, and it's one we satisfy in an endless variety of ways. We form belonging bonds with our coworkers and neighbors and friends. We join clubs, political parties, and social groups structured around interests ranging from cooking to singing to skydiving. And, of course, we gather together in families—traditional families with a mother, a father, and children living under one roof; single-parent families; extended families; communities of believers.

Aside from the basic needs for food, water, and rest, I believe the human need to belong is one of the more important human needs we have. In recent months, the news media have reported on many people who have been forced to leave their families and homes to find jobs in other parts of the country. Significant numbers have returned home again. Apparently they could handle being without money but couldn't handle being without their loved ones and friends. In June of 1976, my family and I moved from Ohio to Arizona. I have since made many close friends in my new home, but I know that the transition would have been far more difficult had not Hester and three of our children been along to provide me with the strength that comes from belonging.

There is a need that transcends even the need to belong, and that is the human need for *love*. Whereas belonging relates to a group, love finds its satisfaction through individual relationships. Some people can get along without satisfying this love-need, especially if their need to belong is fulfilled; this is enough to make life tolerable and afford them some degree of pleasure. But loving and being loved is the greatest of all human joys, the ultimate human experience. We can exist without love; but we are not living fully as human beings without it.

Of these various needs—the basic ones of food, water, rest, and sex and the human ones for control, enjoyment, worth, belonging, and love—which are the most critical? Obviously, we must eat, drink, and sleep in order to survive. But what about the others? Are there any we can do without? Some people make the conscious choice to abstain from sex. Some people never achieve a genuine sense of self-worth. Some people never experience a full love-need satisfaction.

It's true, then, that many don't learn to satisfy all their needs, yet they do stay alive. To really be content, however, *I believe that we need to satisfy each one of our human needs in all areas of our life, and especially our need for love.*

A man or woman who spends his or her life fully satisfying some of their human needs but not others is like a six-cylinder engine running on three cylinders.

Such an engine will perform reasonably well if few demands are placed on it—for example, if it only has to run at moderate speeds on flat roads. But in order to move at higher speeds or climb hills or mountains, it needs all six cylinders to keep from misfiring or breaking down.

Some persons fulfill most if not all of their human needs at work. They like their jobs, are challenged by what they do and can be creative doing it, form belonging bonds with the people they work with, and exercise some degree of control over their work lives. At first glance, they may appear to be purring along on all six cylinders. But are they? Can we really satisfy every one of our human needs at work? What about our love-need? Typically, this is thought to be satisfied not through our jobs but through our social lives.

There are some people, however, who manage to develop close and even intimate friendships with coworkers. They may even carry these friendships into their social lives, although it is not necessary. For them, this is enough to fulfill the love-need and enable them to run on all six cylinders.

Most people, however, simply can't satisfy every one of their human needs at work. But if their social lives aren't going well, they're apt to try. Or they'll forget about the love-need and concentrate on satisfying the others. A contractor I once counseled told me, "The more my wife nags, the more time I spend on the job." He devoted himself to fine-tuning the cylinders that worked rather than fixing the one that didn't—which makes about as much sense as drinking water when you're hungry or lying down to rest when you're thirsty.

Time and again, I have met top management people who were miserable because of what was (or wasn't) going on in their private (social) lives. Their jobs couldn't have been better; their family life couldn't have been worse.

Just as there are some people who can satisfy their human needs at work, there are others who fulfill most of theirs in their individual lives—the time they spend alone with themselves. For example, runners may enjoy running, feel a sense of worth while doing it, and relish the fact that they have so much control over their bodies. They may satisfy their belonging need each time they run a race. But again, what about the love-need?

I am convinced that *the more we are able to satisfy all of our human needs in all areas of our life, the happier and more content we are as human beings.* In other words, the more needs we can fulfill in our work, *and* our social lives, *and* our individual lives, the better off we are. This doesn't mean that we have to fulfill *all* of our human needs in *each* area of our lives. That's too much to expect of a job, a marriage, or our individual alone time.

Let's assume that I like my various jobs (which I do). I have a great deal of control over what I do, take pleasure and derive a sense of worth from them, and feel as if I belong to various groups of people I work for and with. If I didn't also have close friends among my colleagues and clients, that wouldn't be the end of the world—because, in my social life, I'm close to Hester and our children. I walk every day with Hester and interact individually with my children, including semi-weekly target shooting with my son Nelson in the desert. In my individual life, I draw satisfaction from reading, thinking, writing, and running.

Too many of us, though, go through life suffering from partial need-satisfaction. A classic example is the married woman who doesn't work outside the home because there are young children in the family. Rearing children may not be enough to satisfy her various human needs, especially the need to be valued by others in the external world. Once her children are in school, she may decide to get a job. Initially at least, she may do this for economic reasons and then discover along the way that her need to be valued has been greatly enhanced.

It is important to remember that the human needs to be in control of our life, to enjoy ourselves, to feel a sense of self-worth, to belong, and to love *are the same in all of us*. Regardless of our race, religion, or national origin, regardless of our social or economic status, these human needs are as much a part of each of us as are the basic needs for water, food, rest, and sex. To deny them or let them go unfulfilled is to neglect the vehicle that is called the human being.

How do we go about satisfying our human needs? By determining and pursuing specific *wants* and by figuring out what to do with these wants so that our needs will be satisfied. Some wants are simple to define, simple to understand, and reasonably easy to use to meet our needs. We know how to use some from the moment we're born; they're that obvious.

Take food, for example. We learn early in life that only food will take care of that nasty hollow feeling in our stomach. We learn later on, mostly through our parents, which foods are beneficial and which aren't. And we know what to do with food when it's put in front of us.

If I were to tell a four-year-old child, "I'm hungry, and I've got an apple here—what should I do with it?" the child would say, "Eat it." If I persisted in playing dumb by saying, "What do you mean, 'eat it'? Do you mean that I should put the apple under my arm and jump up and down?" The child would laugh. The idea that I didn't know what eating meant would seem silly to the child. *Everyone* knows how to eat!

The child might decide to continue the play-acting by making fun of me. He or she might say, "No, rub your nose with it instead! That's what you should do!" But if I suddenly got serious and said, "Please tell me how to eat this apple," he or she would reply, "You bite into it with your teeth. Then you chew it until it gets soft. Then you swallow it."

What we must do to satisfy our need for love isn't as clear cut. The fighting and bickering and divorces that go on among couples today attest to that.

We have the built-in need and desire to love. We know what to love: other human beings. We don't love sparkplug wrenches or bicycles or kitchen cabinets. But often we don't know *what we must do with other human beings in order to fulfill our love-need.* The need may be apparent, as may the want (a specific person). The behaviors that will result in the want satisfying this human need are another matter, however. Those we must learn.

Most of us, when we marry, behave in ways we honestly believe will fulfill our need for love. We reach into our pasts and dust off everything we ever learned about loving. We do what we think is best. Then, somewhere along the way, we develop various perceptions of what we want, what love is, what works, and what doesn't, and *we program those perceptions in.* We develop behaviors that work or don't work, and we program those in, too. We develop entirely false ideas of what building a relationship is all about.

When we sense that things are going awry, we may start looking for help. We may immerse ourselves in the latest pop psychology or trendy cure. Or, even worse, we may turn to self-help books that focus on teaching us how to satisfy our human needs and achieve happiness *by ourselves.* These books miss the point entirely. And the point they miss is this: *Our need for love can only be fulfilled through and with other human beings.* Loving is never a solo act. Loving never happens unless we work at it through and with another person.

Once we perceive that we have failed at a relationship, the road to learning how to love becomes much harder. The toughest job I have as a counselor is teaching people how to rebuild the confidence they have lost in their ability to love. I often find that they are simply "out of synchronization" with themselves. Their wants, perceptions, and behaviors no longer mesh. Even if they sincerely believe that they want to change, they are resistant and inflexible—locked into false ideas, entrenched in behaviors that make them miserable, and trapped by perceptions that seem rooted in concrete.

One of the first things I do when I begin counseling is to ask the person to list the specific things he or she has and wants. This little exercise can be a terrific eye-opener and a major step toward learning how to build a strong and enduring relationship. For, in the long run, without loving and being loved, life really isn't very satisfying.

* * *

Mary had her job, her marriage to Bill, and her affair with Jim. She didn't want to give up her marriage, but she didn't want to give up Jim, either.

"What do you want to do?" I asked her. "Work at your marriage, leave Bill and move in with Jim, or live alone? Those are the three choices you seem to have."

"I'm not sure I like any of them," she admitted.

"Then why not take the direction it will be easiest to return from later, in case you change your mind?" I suggested. "For example, you can always leave Bill. But if you do, and especially if you then go to live with Jim, going back to Bill will be difficult if not impossible."

Eventually Mary decided to try to work things out with her husband. Happily, she was successful. It wasn't an easy task, but both she and Bill were willing to put some effort into it. That proved to be the key.

* * *

Mark began by listing the things that were important to him: his job as a policeman; Kathy, his wife; his two children; his parents, who lived nearby; playing racquetball, softball, and running.

"Of all these things, which is the most important to you?" I asked.

He hesitated briefly before replying, "Kathy, of course. Without her I'd be lost."

"Are you happy with her now?" I continued.

"No," he replied. Then he grinned. "I guess I should start with her."

"That seems like a good idea."

"Do you really think we have a chance?" he wanted to know.

"Yes, I do," I told him. "But only if you're willing to learn and to work hard at loving Kathy and if she is willing to work hard at loving you."

Later, as Mark was leaving my office, he turned to me and said, "It's strange, but I never knew that loving someone took work. I always thought it was something natural."

2

Taking control of your perceptions

Betty had settled well into her single life. She enjoyed her job as an executive secretary and was pleased with. how her two children were doing at home and in school. She had numerous women friends and a few men friends she dated infrequently. One thing was certain: She never wanted to get married again.

Betty and Lee had been divorced for two years. The divorce had been his idea; he had "needed space." She had been deeply hurt when he left, and it had taken her almost the entire two years to accept the fact that the man she loved no longer loved her. Along the way, she had changed her perception of him. She had gone from perceiving him as someone she cared for to someone she felt passive and indifferent toward. She didn't hate him; she had simply cut him out of her internal world. As far as she was concerned, Lee was the children's father, and that was all.

This change in how she perceived her ex-husband had taken a long time to effect, and it had been painful— so much so that Betty had vowed never to put herself through such pain again. But now the change was full and complete.

Whether or not Lee had changed was immaterial. She had created a new Lee in her mind, a Lee she could tolerate in terms of what she wanted and feel comfort-able with when he came to visit the children. She had adjusted to the circumstances and could handle those times when she had to be in contact with him. Had she not altered her perception of him, she would have been miserable. Because she did, she could live her life and fulfill her various needs in other ways. Her love-need remained partially unsatisfied, but she had learned to live with that, too.

Then one day Lee called and announced that he wanted to get back together again. That's when Betty came to see me.

"He says he realizes he's been a fool," she told me. "He wants to rebuild everything he's lost."

"You have some choices to make," I said. "What are the choices you have?"

She thought for a few moments before answering.

"Well," she finally said, "I suppose I could leave things as they are. Maybe I'll find someone else someday—although I'm not looking for anyone. When I think back to what I went through after Lee left, I don't see how I could risk that with another person."

"What are your other choices?" I prodded.

"I could try just seeing him for a while," she said. "Or I could take him back and take a chance."

"What do you want?" I asked.

"I *want* things to be the way they were before Lee left. But I know that's impossible. And I know Lee isn't the same person he was back then, no matter what he says now."

"Lee might very well be the same person he always was," I said. "It's your perception of him that's changed. You used to see him as someone you loved who loved you. Now you see him simply as the father of your children. Isn't that true?"

"I guess so," she said. "But is he someone I could live with again? I'd have to see him as a lot more than just the children's father for that to happen. I'd have to start loving him all over again. And I'm not sure I could."

* * *

Psychological pain results when there is a difference between *what we want* and *what we perceive*. We have the *need* to love. We have a *want* (a specific person) through whom we believe we can satisfy that need. When we perceive that person as *not* satisfying that need, we hurt.

-16-

We have the capacity to stop hurting by *changing our perceptions and our wants*. That's what Betty had done after Lee left her. For her to take him back into her internal world of wants, she would have to change her perception of him once again. She doubted her abilities to do so, and her fears were understandable. For while the struggle to stay in love is tough enough, the struggle to rebuild love is even tougher.

Like Betty, we can all modify and control how we perceive the people in our lives. We can change a perception that makes us miserable into one we can tolerate. This isn't always easy, but it's often necessary. After my mother and father died, I had to start perceiving them as persons I could not be close to anymore. Had I erected a shrine to my mother or set a place at the table for my father every night, I would have been very unhappy. Those behaviors would have encouraged my perception of them as still present in my life.

Hester is the person—the want—through whom I have chosen to fulfill my love-need. In order for me to be happy with her, my perception of her must conform to what I want: namely, to be happy with her. When it doesn't, one option I have is to change that perception.

Let's say for purposes of illustration that I come home from work one afternoon and Hester starts shouting at me and criticizing me. I am now faced with a decision. I know that I want to avoid perceiving her negatively. For if I do choose that route—if I respond by labeling her mean or hateful—my perception and my want will be at odds. In the midst of the resulting pain, I may *behave* irresponsibly in an attempt to resolve my internal conflict, making what I want more difficult to achieve.

What are my other options? I have three: I could choose to perceive her nonjudgmentally, I could choose not to perceive how she is behaving until later, when the upsetting moments have passed, or I can change how I perceive her actions from negative to positive.

Perceiving her nonjudgmentally requires me to focus my attention away from what she is doing and to see her simply as a person, a human being who happens to be my wife and who will behave differently soon. This perception allows me to preserve within my internal world a picture of the way I want her to be and the way she usually is: loving and caring toward me.

Not perceiving how she is behaving enables me to go on about my business in the house without acknowledging her shouting and criticism. It may mean that I have to avoid her for a while, but this is preferable to my having to deal with her while she is upset.

The ability to not perceive what is going on around us comes naturally to most of us. When I was a newspaper reporter in the fifties, I was assigned to visit an illegal gambling operation in a nearby town. Hester accompanied me. On the following day, I showed her the story I had written. In it was a reasonably thorough account (or so I thought) of what I had observed: the gambling tables, the physical setup, the various precautions the owners had taken to avoid discovery.

When Hester had finished reading my story, she commented, "But you didn't mention the *types* of people who were gambling there."

"What do you mean?" I asked, mystified.

"Well, here's one example," she went on. "Those people who were waiting to play bingo downstairs were all in their sixties. Couldn't you tell how you and I stood out?"

We were both in our twenties at the time. I hadn't even noticed the difference.

We also have the ability to take what has the potential for becoming a negative perception and turn it into a positive one. In other words, we can, if we choose, keep our perceptions in tune with our wants.

I have a dear friend who does this constantly. She chooses to see the world in such a way as to make living a joyful experience. And that, I believe, is the secret to being a happy person. Not long ago, she gave birth to her first child. Her delivery was difficult. Toward the end, her physician urged her to push, adding, "Work like you're rowing a boat." She replied, "I've rowed boats, and this isn't like rowing a boat." Then she burst into laughter. The doctor started laughing, everyone else in the delivery room started laughing, and soon she delivered her son.

Of course, we also have the ability to take a positive perception and turn it into a negative one. For example, a young woman who is engaged to be married may perceive her future husband as easy-going and re-laxed—qualities she likes. Later, after they've been mar-ried for a while and have experienced the financial dif-ficulties most newlyweds face, she may see him as lazy and unconcerned about the family finances. He may not have really changed a bit, but her perception of him certainly did.

When I continually work to maintain a positive per-ception of Hester, it is much easier for me to remain close to her—where I want to be. Because I'm in the habit of seeing her as a loving, caring person, *it is much easier for me to return to that perception after those times when I've chosen to perceive her nonjudgmentally or not to perceive her behavior at all.* This process becomes easier still when I avoid forming negative perceptions altogether. For, once formed, they're tempting to return to in times of con-flict—as Betty discovered.

*   *   *

Betty decided to take Lee back and hope for the best. They began by spending short periods of time to-gether—quality time. Then the trouble started.

During the next several weeks, Betty tried to reinstate her positive perception of her husband. But whenever Lee behaved in a way that didn't fit her expectations or wants, she would revert to a negative perception of him. The slightest mishap, the smallest infraction, and sud-denly her perception of what she wanted (a loving Lee) and what she perceived (an uncaring Lee) would be at odds. And that would bring on the pain she had only recently managed to rid herself of and had vowed never again to experience.

"Things were much better before Lee and I got back together again," she told me one day. "Then everything was under control. I was happy. The kids were happy. Now we're up one day and down the next. Frankly, I don't think things are going to work out between us."

As it happened, they didn't. Eventually Betty reviewed her choices and made the one she felt she could best live with: living without Lee. Not all marriages can be rebuilt. And when one partner has firmly decided that going it alone is less painful than staying together, there is little that can be done to change his or her mind.

A fifty-three-year-old woman I know sells her own handmade jewelry with her daughter and has a thriving business, but not enough to support the two of them. She is married to a man who, though not mean, is unwilling to do anything with her and spends his time watching television. Since, financially, divorce was out of the question, she changed how she perceived her husband from hate to indifference, which reduced considerably the pain caused by the difference between what she wanted (warm relationship) and what she perceived (total rejection). Since she is fulfilling her needs through her work and children, she can tolerate the marriage.

* * *

Our perceptual system takes the energy of the world around us and translates it in such a way that we can use it to fulfill our needs. *The only real meaning anything outside of us has to us is the meaning we give it.* The typewriter I am using to write this book would have little or no meaning to a starving child. At best, he or she would see it as a curiosity. To me, however, it has a great deal of meaning as the vehicle I use to express my thoughts.

My father was a stamp collector. His hobby satisfied his needs for enjoyment, for belonging (to a group of stamp-collecting friends), and for worth (he was known for specializing in British West Indies and precancelled stamps). When he died, my brother and sisters and I decided to sell his collection. None of us wanted it; it didn't fulfill any of our needs. We perceived the collection in a vastly different way than our father had.

Our perceptual system plays an important role in our relationships. As long as I perceive Hester as someone I love who loves me, my behavior toward her would reflect that perception—namely kind and loving. But if I were to perceive her as cold and indifferent toward me, I would find it very difficult to deal in a loving way with her. *The key is to maintain the habit of continually building positive perceptions of the persons to whom you want to be close even, at times, in spite of what they do.*

Recently a friend told me this story: Her husband came home from work one day, tired and upset, and headed off to take a hot bath. For some reason, there was no hot water, and he stormed out of the bathroom in an even worse mood. My friend had spent years building strong, positive perceptions of her husband, and she chose to view his behavior nonjudgmentally. Instead of getting angry in return, she put her arm around him and said, "Honey, the bed is nice and warm—why not lie down and rest for a while?" He awoke an hour later, relaxed and cheerful.

Our ability to control our perceptions of those we love is a primary factor in determining how happy we are with them. This is not always easy, but then I said loving takes work.

* * *

Sally was in her early thirties and had been married to Phil, her third husband, for less than a year. Her first two marriages had ended when her husbands had become involved with other women.

"I just don't trust Phil," she told me. "Yet I don't have any reason not to. I get so angry with him!"

"What happened the last time you got angry with him?" I asked.

"I screamed at him and ran out of the house," she said. "It seems like that's all I'm doing lately. We can't talk anymore. It's a constant battle."

"Is your angry behavior helping your relationship?"

"No, but I don't know what to do. Whenever I see him, I get furious."

We worked together to come up with a plan to change Sally's behavior. Essentially, the plan was for her to walk away from Phil whenever she sensed her anger building, to do something calming, and then to return to him when she felt better. Over the next few weeks, she tried this with some success. But she still continued to have problems with her perception of her husband.

Then one day she burst into my office and exclaimed, "I did it! I really did it!"

"Did what?" I asked.

Her story poured out in a rush.

"Last Sunday, I asked Phil to go bike riding with me, and he said that he had to go over to a friend's house to help her fix her car. Immediately I started thinking, 'He's going to see this woman for another reason. The car is just an excuse.' I then said to Phil, 'Well, if your friend is more important than I am, go ahead.' I ran out of the house, got on my bike, and rode away.

"I was really angry. Then, all of a sudden, I remembered what you had told me—that I could control how I perceived Phil. I could perceive him positively, or negatively, or indifferently, or not at all. I realized that Phil wasn't making me angry—I was choosing to be angry by changing my perception of him from positive to negative.

"I decided to try concentrating on my ride. I felt the breeze and the warm sunshine on my face. I looked around and noticed some children playing in a yard, spoke to them, and they smiled back at me. I started feeling better. Before I knew it, I was really having a good time. I was happy!

"As I turned to go home, I began thinking about Phil again and imagining what he was doing with that woman.

Then I thought, 'This is silly. How do I know he's doing anything except fixing her car? And even if he is, how does my thinking about it help me?' I could feel myself beginning to anger again, and I decided to notice the breeze and feel the warm sunshine in my face. I stopped getting angry.

"I made up my mind not to say anything mean to Phil when he came home. I would just say hi and kiss him. That would make me feel good. If Phil chose to be angry with me, that would be his problem.

"When I got home, I took a shower, put on something light, and began to fix lunch for myself. I thought, 'Since Phil isn't here, I'm not about to fix anything for him.' And then I thought, 'There you go again, Sally! Getting even!' So I decided to fix him something, too, and put it in the refrigerator for him.

"When Phil walked in the door, I could tell that he didn't know what to expect. He half smiled at me, and I smiled back. 'Hi,' I said, 'want something to eat?' He came over and kissed me, and I kissed him back and gave him a hug.

"Just then the phone rang. I answered it, and the voice at the other end said, 'Is this Sally?' I said it was. 'Who's this?' I asked. 'It's Maggie, Phil's friend. I wanted to call and thank you for letting me borrow your husband for a while. I needed someone to help me fix the engine in my car, and Phil's the only person I know who understands how to do it!'

"So that's what he really was doing after all," Sally concluded, grinning. "Helping a friend fix her car!"

* * *

Not only can we control our perceptions by the behaviors we choose, but this idea can be taken one step further. Not only is behavior the control of perception; *it can also be the consequence of perception* as we shall see later. We behave in ways intended to change our perceptions to how we want things to be. Often, the way we *want* something to be may not be the way we perceive it to be. Conscious of the disparity between the two, we will direct our efforts toward satisfying our wanting perception.

A behavior has three components: what we *do*, what we *think*, and what we *feel*. The first two components directly affect the third. In fact, our feelings are a natural outgrowth of our actions and thoughts.

We can create good feelings for ourselves by changing what we do and what we think. This is what Sally learned. Before, whenever she thought about Phil having an affair with another woman (which he never did), this perception of her husband cheating on her conflicted with what she wanted—namely, a happy marriage. And this conflict between her want and perception created stressful pain within Sally.

On the day of her great discovery, Sally had felt herself getting angry with Phil. Rather than continue her angry behavior, she had forced herself to *do* certain things: enjoy her bike ride; fix Phil something to eat; greet him with a smile and a hug when he returned. She had also forced herself to *think* certain thoughts: what a lovely day it was; how nice it would be if she made Phil's lunch and put it in the refrigerator for him; and so on. Those actions and thoughts had created good feelings within her. They had reinforced her perception of the way she wanted things to be between Phil and herself.

Changing behaviors to perceive what we want is hard work, and it doesn't happen overnight. With practice, though, it will happen. This was evident in a letter Sally wrote to me not long afterward that reflected on the struggle she was going through:

It's hard to let go of old behaviors. There are times when I try to help the situation between us and end up getting depressed or frustrated. But I'm beginning to see that my behavior doesn't depend on his responses. It depends on *my* doing something constructive and good.

A couple of times I haven't wanted to kiss Phil good morning, but I did it anyway with a "what the hell" attitude, and it was amazing how that made me forget whatever it was I was upset about. Now whenever I kiss him good morning or good night, I feel good, not because I did it for him but because *I did it for me.* It's almost like I'm giving *me* the kiss, even though I'm planting it on him!

. . . I finally know what I need to do to make a marriage work, and I know how to deal with me. I'm frightened at times, but it gets easier every day.

When Sally married Phil, she'd already had two husbands who had been unfaithful to her. The fact that she suspected Phil of doing the same was understandable. But that didn't make it helpful. By the time Sally came to see me, her negative (and false) perceptions of Phil were well on their way to destroying that marriage, too. Luckily, she saw that her negative perceptions weren't helping, and she became open to working on *any* plan that would improve her relationship with Phil. She was willing to be flexible, and that made all the difference.

We human beings are more flexible than we think. We are constantly making decisions and reasoning things through. Yet despite our inherent flexibility, we lock ourselves into programmed behaviors. We eat the same foods, drive the same routes to work, and talk about the same things day after day. When faced with a conflict between what we perceive and what we want, we tend to react in patterned ways: We get headaches, we get angry, we get depressed, we take a drink.

We also lock ourselves into programmed perceptions, and these can be more restrictive and destructive than programmed behaviors. These perceptions restrict our behaviors because our behaviors flow from our perceptions. They also prevent us from seeing people objectively.

For example, let's assume for a moment that I have a negative perception of Orientals and have decided that they're not dependable. If I should meet someone from Japan, that prejudice would stand in the way of my developing any positive perceptions of the person's decency. If the person should happen to be a man, and that man should happen to be my daughter's boyfriend, I would be apt to respond to or behave toward him by rejecting him out of hand, causing pain for myself. All because of a negative perception of Orientals.

In a way, Sally had programmed a negative perception against husbands. Because of her past experiences, she viewed them as untrustworthy. Never mind what Phil was really like; she perceived him as someone who would run off with another woman whenever he had the chance. How much better off we are—and how much our abilities to deal with the world are enhanced—when we keep from forming negative perceptions.

Sally's case exemplifies yet another problem that occurs when we form perceptions of others that don't conform to our wants: We retaliate. In the midst of our pain—which we create within ourselves as stress—we strike out at those we love in an attempt to control what they are doing. Or we avoid them in the belief that close contact is worse than no contact at all. This locks us even more firmly into a conflict mode, making reconciliation difficult if not impossible. To open the door to reconciliation with Phil and the happy marriage she desired, Sally first had to learn to control her perceptions of her husband. She couldn't control *him*: only her perceptions of him. Out of her new behaviors flowed new positive perceptions from which flowed new positive behaviors. Remember, behaviors control perceptions.

There is no way to know whether our perception of another person is objectively accurate or not; it is accurate only for ourselves. Often, a perception we have of someone may be completely different from the person's own perception of himself or herself. I may view a friend as too talkative in a crowd; he may view himself as possessing social skills and as adept at the art of conversation.

The point here is that what we perceive isn't always what others perceive. For example, my son Nelson is a gunsmith. He sees a Smith & Wesson revolver as a beautiful piece of art, a finely constructed tool that enables him to enjoy the sport of target shooting. Many others see the same revolver as a dangerous and ugly weapon. The hardest thing to understand is that since everything outside of me is energy and what is in my mind gives it meaning, the way I perceive the world is quite different from others.

We become very possessive of our perceptions of the world. We don't want to give them up, and we look for others to reinforce them: When they don't, we get defensive. For instance, I might perceive a particular woman as sensuous. If I were to tell this to a friend and he were to disagree with me and insist that she was plain, I would hold up my perception of her as the "correct" one. If on the other hand my friend concurred with me that, yes, she *was* sensuous, I would take this as further proof that *she was that way.*

We tend to assign our perceptions to the persons or objects we perceive. We forget that our perceptions are *in us*—in *our* heads—and though related to others' behavior, these perceptions are not an exact reflection of them as human beings. In short, we create a person's reality. If my friend agreed with my opinion of the woman, I'd be delighted. But this would *mean* nothing more than that I'd found someone whose perception matched mine.

I know for a fact that I have clung to some perceptions for years, despite my friends' best efforts to rid me of them. For example, I have always thought that many paintings by Picasso were downright ugly. Time and again, I have been told that authorities in the field of art consider Picasso one of the world's greatest painters. My friends have patiently shown me, over and over, what it is about his works that exemplify creativity and genius. Yet I *still* perceive them to be ugly, and I probably always will. Whenever someone tries to tell me otherwise, I simply *filter out* whatever he or she is saying and thus refuse to allow the perceptions of others to enter and become a part of my world.

Filtering out the opinions and perceptions of others is something we do throughout our lives. How many of us have been warned by close friends to go slowly in a love affair? We may listen, we may even nod as if we're agreeing, yet all the while we're convinced that our perception of our intended love *must* be right. So we say, "You've just got to get to *know* her. You don't *know* her yet; when you do, you'll change your mind." What we're really saying, of course, is, "You've got to perceive her as *I* do." *It just becomes much easier to deal with the world by filtering out certain perceptions and perceiving only those things about others (and things) that conform to what we want to perceive.*

It's hard to avoid finding fault with a perception that doesn't fit our own. It seems so *obvious* that the way we perceive something is the way it really *is*. Time and again, we encounter evidence that our perceptions are not the perceptions of the world, and rather than face it we just filter it out.

Sometimes we hold so tenaciously to our perceptions that we lose our ability to discriminate between fact and fantasy. Often our perceptions themselves are little more than fantasies. Many couples go into marriage bearing fantasy perceptions of each other. They believe that living together will be a series of joyful events and a totally heavenly experience. What happens when the fantasy encounters the fact of actually living together, and the difference between fantasy and fact is significant? These persons hurt. If they relax their hold on their fantasy perceptions, if they change their behavior so as to create new perceptions that are closer to fact, then the marriage will have a chance at survival. But if they persist in their fantasy perceptions and the behaviors that reinforce them, they'll more likely than not be miserable with each other.

Keeping a marriage intact requires flexibility on the part of both partners. Each must be flexible enough to change his or her perception of the other, to form different perceptions at different stages of the relationship. Interestingly, however, the perception that binds a couple over a period of years is the one that brought them together in the first place: specifically, "I perceive this person as someone I *want*."

A wanting perception is characterized by certain behaviors. As long as we want someone, our behavior toward that person is directed at making him or her a part of us and our lives. We do nice things for him or her, show signs of affection, and are generally careful of what we say and do.

Wanting something and the behavior that flows from the wanting are both activated only when our human or basic needs demand fulfilling. And these needs demand continual satisfaction. For example, for me to fulfill my love-need through Hester, I must continually perceive her as someone I want, and *I must continue to behave toward her as someone through whom I want to fulfill my love-need.* If I stop this perception and this behavior, my love-need will go unsatisfied or I will begin to look elsewhere for satisfaction. For it is only when we *want* something that we *act* on it; and it is only when we *act* on the object of our want that it can satisfy the need.

Unfortunately, we often perceive our loved ones as objects to be possessed, to be with, or just to have around but not acted on. And so, once we have the person we wanted—once we are married to that person—our behavior often changes. We form a new perception of him or her as someone we *have*. The behaviors that flowed from the wanting perception cease. So does the effort we put into getting the person. *And herein lies the main reason why marriages fall apart: We stop working at them.*

I'll illustrate this idea with another example. Let's say I want to buy a car. I spend all my time going from one automobile agency to another in search of the car I want. I read books and newspaper ads about cars. My energies are focused on getting the car I want. Once I have found it, these behaviors end. The car is now something I have, and I can move on to other concerns.

When a husband and wife continue to perceive each other as someone they *want*—to live with, to be happy with, to share their thoughts and activities with, to meet their needs—they will keep growing closer and their marriage will keep growing stronger. The alive, active behaviors that flow from the wanting perception will be evident in their alive, active marriage. The behaviors that go into a having perception are another matter. With a having perception of someone, we tend to take that person for granted. We behave indifferently toward him or her. We mistakenly assume that our love-need has been met since we now *have* that person. We forget that the love-need requires continual satisfaction all our lives and can never be satiated permanently; that we must give it constant attention by working continually at the relationship. And we become blind to the fact that this is true for our partner as well.

Just because we get someone we want doesn't mean that we can relax and take it easy. Instead, we must continually work at maintaining the level of effortful activity it took to achieve our goal and initially meet our love-need. In short, *we must continue to perceive them as persons we want and continually act on them to satisfy our love-need.*

When I first met Hester, I began perceiving her as someone I wanted to be happy with. Then we got married, and I quickly discovered that I had no idea of what I had to do to keep fulfilling my love-need through her. I learned that I had to continue to perceive her as someone I wanted and to work at our relationship around the clock. One thing I discovered is that it's often best to keep as many of our perceptions as nonjudgmental or indifferent as we can. The more things I look for to perceive critically about Hester, the more difficult it will be for me to deal with her. If I am critical of a particular dress she owns, I am going to choose to be upset every time she puts it on. If I am critical of her driving, I am going to choose to be tense and irritable every time I ride with her.

What if I chose to perceive Hester as someone I didn't care for or even hated? This would be obvious to her from the way I treated her. If she wanted to keep our marriage together anyway, she could respond by asking me to do things with her—take a walk in the evening, play a card game. She might even be more sexually accommodating to me. All of these behaviors would be directed toward reinforcing her perception of me as someone she wanted to be married to and happy with. But what if I continued with my disruptive and abusive behavior? What choices would be left to her then?

She would have three options: to live with the misery; to separate from me or divorce me; or to spend more time with me alone in the hope of repairing the damage that I was causing. If the third option did not work— if I remained unresponsive and stubbornly persisted in my negative behavior toward her—she would have only the first two options. And if the pain of living with me proved greater than her perception of the alternative— the pain of *not* living with me—she would probably give up and leave me. It isn't enough for one partner to be willing to work at a marriage. Both must expend sufficient effort and make a commitment to preserving and strengthening the relationship. Yet how many times we observe one partner blaming the other for something, making it more difficult for the other person to *want* to work at the relationship.

Whenever a couple approaches me and asks if I will counsel them, I begin by posing one question to them: "Do you *want* to work at your marriage?" It may be hard at first for both (or either) of them to answer honestly. Eventually, however, they will have to decide, or it will be revealed in what they do. If they aren't willing to work at rebuilding their married life together, then there's no point in going on. Regardless of the reason for trying— whether it's fear of being alone, belief that one partner can't make it financially without the other, or a conviction that they'll never find anyone else to love—if they

-31-

are both willing to work at the marriage, then we proceed. I never ask why. It has no therapeutic value, and pursuing the reasons could be disastrous.

Negative perceptions wreak havoc in all areas of our lives. If we constantly see those around us as stupid, uncaring, manipulative, or whatever, we'll find it very hard to deal with them. I once counseled a woman who was highly critical of her coworkers. I asked her to spend a week just perceiving them as persons, without making judgments about them. The next time we met, she reported, "It's strange, but everyone seems to be acting a lot nicer to me lately!" Maybe they were, and maybe they weren't. What mattered was that the woman now had a new and more positive perception of the persons she worked with.

There is one final point about perceptions. We know what our own perceptions are, but we can't know what another person's perceptions are and we can only tell that their perceptions have changed when we see a decided change in the pattern of their behavior over an extended period of time. Even then, we can't read our partner's mind or expect him or her to read ours.

Many people have come to me insisting that their spouse's behavior has changed overnight. Suddenly, they claim, their husband or wife has gone from being warm and caring to being cold or even cruel. The truth of the matter is that major changes rarely take place all at once. They may seem to, though, if a couple has stopped paying attention to each other. Most changes, though, begin to take place within the perceptual system or our internal world of wants and thus are not always discernible.

* * *

When Barbara and John came to see me, their marriage was in serious trouble. John in particular couldn't understand why Barbara was acting as she was. "I thought we were doing fine!" he told me.

In private, Barbara admitted to me that she had become tired of John's expectations of her as a housewife. In her mind, that was the least of her roles. She was an advertising executive who had been promoted several times. John, a contractor, still saw her as someone who was supposed to do all the cleaning and cooking.

Over the years, Barbara had begun meeting more and more of her needs through her job. It gave her a sense of worth. She had found many close friends, a group to whom she belonged. She was able to exercise a significant amount of control over what she was doing. As her satisfaction with her work increased, she perceived her need to remain married to John as less important than it formerly was. When she started traveling for her company, she became intimately involved with another man.

Meanwhile John became increasingly involved in his own work. As the construction business began to slow down, he spent more time alone on the job. For a while, he didn't mind. Then, gradually, he became more dependent on his marriage. He was meeting so few of his needs through work that he began looking to Barbara as the person who could satisfy more of them.

During what was in effect a transition period in their marriage, John behaved pretty much the same as he always had. He was too busy to notice the subtle changes in Barbara's behavior. When John learned of his wife's affair, he was profoundly shaken.

John could not have perceived Barbara's lack of need-fulfillment in their relationship. He could only perceive her *behaviors*. As long as he *perceived* these to be fairly constant, he assumed that his partner's love for him had stayed the same. He was totally unaware of the subtle, long-term shift that was taking place both in her perceptual system and in what she wanted. He hadn't perceived the subtle change in her behaviors from a generous, enthusiastic lover to someone who performed the functions of her wifely "duties" with mechanical actions.

John wanted desperately to work at rebuilding the marriage; initially, at least, Barbara wasn't sure if she did. Ultimately, Barbara's need-satisfactions from her job appealed to her such that reconciliation with her husband became less and less desirable. John continued to work at the marriage for several months until Barbara filed for divorce.

Perceptions in another don't change easily. Talking to our spouse does little good unless we also *do* things with our spouse and begin to change our own behavior toward him or her. Only then is there a *chance* of change. The actual experience of doing something together is more effective than talking. Even then, however, our spouse must *want to change.*

Our perceptual system plays a major role in how we get along with others. Like it or not, we control our perceptions of the world and ourselves. We can change these perceptions, and we can change our behaviors— but we can't change the way others behave, whether they like us or not, what they do for us, and what they allow us to do for them. Their perceptions and wants are hidden from us. And when they do reveal them, we are frequently surprised. We may try to control other people and bring them around to our way of perceiving and thinking. In the end, however, we are left with this truth: All we really have control over is what *we* perceive, what *we* want, and what *we* do.

3

Forming positive perceptions: the key to staying in love

Recently a friend came to me with good news. Her mother had found happiness with her fifth husband. One of the previous husbands had died, and she had divorced the other three, but the fifth looked promising. "For as long as I can remember," my friend told me, "my mother has been miserable. You know how she criticized each of her other four husbands. But now she laughs all the time, and the two of them are always busy doing things together. I don't know what happened, but I think she found a winner!"

The mystery of what makes one marriage work and another fail has puzzled me ever since I taught high school back in the middle sixties. The young students, especially the girls, would ask me about marriage and love and sex and what they were all about. I was married, I loved Hester, and I enjoyed our sex life together, but I still didn't understand why and how marriage worked. I did my best to come up with answers to my students' questions, crossing my fingers in the hope that I wasn't leading them astray.

Today, some twenty years later, I think I have a good idea of what a couple must do to stay together happily over the long term. To begin with, they must recognize that problems, no matter how serious, do not cause the downfall of a marriage. Instead, problems are merely symptomatic of a marriage that is weak at its core. *Every* couple has difficulties or relational conflicts somewhere along the way. To put it simply, some have the strength to combat and correct them while others don't.

I do not agree with the approach some counselors take to helping their clients with their marriage problems. More often than not, they start off by asking their clients to list and describe the problems they are having. Then they sit back and listen to a litany of complaints: not enough money; a meddling mother-in-law; a teenage son or daughter who has become disruptive or disobedient; sexual inadequacy or dysfunction; an unhappy childhood; an alcoholic mother; an abusive father. The counselors *accept* whatever their clients say and proceed at that point to effect a "cure." And what is that "cure"? *Talking things out.*

Some therapists are convinced that airing feelings will somehow make them go away. They fail to realize that while a couple is hurling accusations at each other, the fire of their negative feelings is consuming what little love they may have left. Too many counselors spend hours and weeks and months dragging their clients through the past. Couples are forced to review and relive miseries they suffered during childhood, miseries they have suffered during their marriage, horrible things they have done and said to each other, and wrongs they have committed, whether consciously or unconsciously. It is an arduous process—and, to me, a wasteful and damaging one, for it only serves to reinforce negative perceptions which must be changed to effect reconciliation.

I know couples who have spent literally years in therapy, and I find it amazing that they're able to endure such pain. I recall one couple in particular who, acting under their therapist's instructions, subjected themselves to a battery of psychological tests. When the results came back, they were told that they were badly mismatched. What a burden to place on two people who were struggling to rebuild an unhappy marriage!

Saving a marriage requires doing, not talking; dealing with the present, not living in the past; and practical alternatives, not theory.

As noted earlier, we all have human needs that drive us. Our wants are the things (or people) through which we believe our needs can be met. Our perceptual system translates the outside world and makes sense of it so that we can use it to get what we want. And when getting what we want satisfies our needs, we are happy. Conversely, when getting what we want *doesn't* satisfy our needs, we are unhappy. Thinking that something will satisfy our needs doesn't necessarily mean that it will. For example, if I decided that a piece of chalk would meet my hunger-need, I'd learn differently as soon as I tried to eat it.

We form positive, negative, or indifferent perceptions of the people and things around us. A positive or negative perception gets us personally involved with whatever we are perceiving. An indifferent judgment, on the other hand, means that we are ignoring it, and for whatever reason, not becoming involved in it.

I perceive many things every day that affect me very little because I choose to perceive them indifferently. The cactus in the front yard; a rock on the ground; a chair in the house; a light bulb—to me, they're simply there. I don't have to deal with them in any real sense. But if one day I were to form a negative perception of the cactus, for instance—if I were to decide that it looked awful in the yard, that I just couldn't stand it, and that it had to go—I would cut it down (behave) in order to reduce the pain caused by the difference between what I wanted (an attractive cactus in my yard) and my negative perception. I would have to get involved with the cactus for as long as it took to cut it down and haul it away. Avoiding a negative perception of the cactus, in other words, saves me a lot of trouble. The point I am making here is that *the more people and objects we perceive indifferently, the fewer concerns we have and the more manageable our lives become.*

Once I climbed into Hester's car and noticed that the floor and seats were full of debris—papers, kids' clothing, and the like. I keep my own car relatively spotless, and having to shove aside a pile of stuff before I could get comfortable in hers, I chose to get irritated. So I said, "Doesn't all this mess bother you?" And she replied, calmly and patiently, "I just don't let it concern me. There are a lot of things I don't get concerned about. If I did, I never would have been able to raise eight children." My negative judgment of the way she cared for her car had led me to attempt to change her. Instead, I should have been working at changing my own perception. For she was absolutely right—and I was well-rebuked.

Needless to say, if we perceived everyone and everything indifferently our lives would be very dull and our needs wouldn't be met. So we choose to perceive certain persons and things either positively, because they satisfy our wants and ultimately our needs, or negatively, because they conflict with our wants. And we interact with those persons and things. We just have to keep a reasonable balance between those things we choose to see indifferently and those we want to interact with.

When I first met Hester, I thought to myself, "Now there's the person through whom I want to satisfy my need for love." Fortunately, she had the same idea about me as I had about her. But what if she hadn't perceived me in that way? Then what I wanted (to be together and happy with her) and what I perceived (her rejecting me) would have created a perceptual difference in my brain, or pure pain or stress. That in turn would have activated my behavioral system to try to change what I perceived into what I wanted to perceive.

We are all driven, then, by needs that motivate us; wants that we believe will satisfy our needs; perceptions of the people and things around us that are formulated in terms of whether they conform to our wants; and behaviors directed toward controlling and changing those perceptions.

Permanent Love maintains that spending quality time alone together doing specific activities can make a marriage stronger and better. And the reason for this is: When you spend quality time with your partner, *you are altering your perception of him or her.* Your behavior is causing you to perceive your partner more positively and to satisfy your need for love. It seems that what makes it difficult to change our behavior toward others is our tendency to program both our perceptions and behaviors.

That we have programmed perceptions is evident in our tendency to accept new perceptions only if they conform to ones we already have and to reject or filter them out, if they don't. For example, let's say that I perceive Hester as hateful and uncaring. If she stops on the way home especially to buy avocados for me—which she knows I like—I might choose to filter out any perception of this act as kind or caring and, instead, criticize her for not buying jack cheese—which she also knows I like. Or I may choose to perceive it indifferently or ignore it. If she decides to leave me alone until I come out of my bad mood, I'll probably accuse her of ignoring me. In any event, I will not allow any perception of her as a considerate person to enter my thinking; to do so would contradict my programmed, negative perception of her. In other words, we tend to ignore those things persons do when their actions don't conform to how we are presently perceiving them. It is easier to act in such a way that will confirm our perceptions.

If I am perceiving Hester negatively, I will gather thoughts and impressions of her that contribute to the negative perception. I'll tell myself things like, "She's no good," "She doesn't love me and never has," and so on. I will look at everything she does, moving from positive to negative perceptions of all her actions. Like the way she disciplines one of our children ("She's being too critical"); the way she drives ("Why doesn't she brake sooner?"); the way she pays the monthly bills

("What's the matter with her? Can't she perform a simple subtraction?"); the way she addresses an envelope ("Her handwriting is getting worse every day"). When she does something that doesn't fit the negative picture of her I'm busy perceiving, I'll simply filter it out or perceive it indifferently.

The more I filter out Hester's "good" behavior and convince myself that she doesn't care for me, the more miserable I will become. My perception of her has nothing to do with the woman I married; and furthermore, she can do nothing to change that perception for me. It is *mine*, and it is up to me to change it so that we can get along once again. But to admit to a wrong perception of someone is hard to do and demands strength and self-confidence.

Many couples seem to work hard at developing negative perceptions of each other; and those perceptions aren't always unfounded. My point is this: No matter what our spouse is like, we must deal with *our* perception of him or her if we want our relationship to grow stronger and more loving.

We also seem to have programmed wants as well as programmed perceptions. We cling to some of our wants as if they're the answer to our most desperate prayers— whether or not satisfying them really fulfills our needs. Even when our perceptual system tells us to modify a particular want and gives us specific information to prove that we should modify it, we refuse to listen. We even concoct fantasy wants and hang our hopes on them.

Most of us are adept at creating fantasy wants. A young man might say to himself, "If only I could be married to that woman, I'd be happy." Would he? Of course not. What makes us happy is the effort we put into loving someone over a period of time. Nevertheless, we all pursue fantasy wants at different stages of our lives. We become convinced that living in *this* house, earning *that* amount of money, winning *this* award, getting *that* promotion, or owning *this* car will make our dreams of happiness come true. Advertising constantly plants new fantasy wants in our minds. If we buy a certain product, it tells us, we'll be sexier, healthier, more popular, more attractive, more successful, or whatever the implied promise may be. We're so inundated by advertising that we become obsessed in trying to satisfy our needs through these fantasy wants. A TV ad may simply create a fantasy perception which gives the illusion of satisfying a human need. If we respond to the ad by believing it will somehow help us satisfy a need, we create a fantasy want and buy the product.

We also have programmed behavior patterns. I know, for instance, that I get dressed in a certain way nearly every day. I put on my clothes in essentially the same order. *We humans are not designed to consider every act we perform*; if we did, we'd soon get bogged down in paralyzing details and find ourselves unable to function. *It's more convenient to form a perception of how we want to perceive ourselves to be*—in my case, dressed each morning—*and then develop a set of programmed behaviors to satisfy that perception of ourselves. Thus, we learn and develop patterns of behaviors when we want to perceive things, ourselves, or others in a certain way.*

Some psychologists mistakenly believe these patterns of behavior to be conditioned responses. That we cannot help ourself, that the world caused us to be this way, is simply not true. These programmed behaviors are learned and then intentionally programmed by a person who is trying to fulfill his or her needs—a person with varying wants and perceptions, and a person with a highly flexible behavioral system with a seemingly infinite number of choices available—for which that person is totally responsible.

Another example of programmed behaviors was when I first drove a foreign car, about ten years ago. I had rented it on a rainy day at Chicago's O'Hare Airport. As soon as I climbed in, I knew that I wanted to perceive the windshield wipers working so I executed the programmed behaviors that always started the windshield wipers in my American-made car. But pushing the knob

I had programmed to push didn't get the desired result. Then—and *only* then—did I become fully conscious of what I was doing. After spending a few moments talking to myself and becoming increasingly frustrated (none of the behaviors got the wipers going), I opened the glove compartment, pulled out the owner's manual, and read through it until I learned where the windshield wiper switch was. *We are rarely conscious of what we are actually doing, only of what we perceive happening. That is why we have to examine how we have programmed our behaviors.* Incidentally, this illustration not only shows that we have programmed behaviors; it also shows that we can *change* them if need be.

If we have programmed behaviors that determine how we perform our daily routines and how we act toward the objects around us, then it stands to reason that *we have programmed behaviors in dealing with others* too, and that *these behaviors reflect what we want to perceive.* When I first met Hester, I perceived her as sweet and loving. I wanted to perceive her in that way. Once we were married, I began developing a number of behaviors that reflected my perception. Today many of these are so entrenched in my being that I hardly think about them anymore. I greet her warmly when she comes home after an absence, no matter how brief; I touch her often, kiss her, and pat her when I walk by; I help her prepare the evening meal and make the bed with her in the morning. I don't plan or even consider every one of these behaviors; I simply do them. I've literally programmed them into my behavioral system.

But what if I perceive Hester as unloving and cold? Most of us have programmed negative behaviors to flow from our negative perceptions. We create negative behavior patterns because we believe at the time it's the best way to get others to conform to the way we want to perceive them. So I might choose programmed behaviors such as shouting, sulking, or giving her the cold shoulder. I might kick the cat or yell at the kids. Strangely enough, we choose these hurtful kinds of behaviors when we're desperate to perceive happiness in our lives. These actions usually make things worse, but we continue to do them anyway.

By labeling certain behaviors "programmed," I don't mean to imply that we're not responsible for them. We certainly are; no one else programs our behaviors for us. *We choose our own behaviors.* And once programmed, we rarely evaluate the effectiveness of what we do, even when it doesn't get us what we want.

And what kinds of behaviors do we most frequently choose? *Those we believe will change the behaviors of the people around us to conform to the way we want to perceive them.* To put it more simply and somewhat less kindly, we try to manipulate them. By doing so, we set ourselves an impossible task. For we cannot change the behaviors of others no matter how hard we try. Instead, we should be working at changing our perceptions of them. For perceptions are much, much easier to change than behaviors. We can alter the way we view someone far more readily than we can alter the way we act toward and around him or her. As we succeed in altering our perceptions, our programmed behaviors will change to new ones. We don't often stop to realize that we learn both positive *and* negative behaviors, and we program ourselves with both. We know how to be nice as surely as we know how to be nasty. Once we switch our perception of another from negative to positive, *we will switch to new behaviors that will mirror that quality.*

Out of positive perceptions will flow positive programmed behavior including warm feelings. When we feel good about someone, it merely reflects the predominant perceptions we have of them, day in and day out. In fact, *the key to staying in love lies in forming and maintaining positive perceptions of those we love.* When we do this, we not only behave in ways that are constructive to our relationships but we also become skilled at handling the difficult times, primarily through maintaining our positive perceptions from which will continue to flow effective behaviors. The persons we love won't always behave in ways that are pleasing to us. But when they don't, we can choose to perceive their behaviors positively or we can choose to see them indifferently; we can filter them out and refuse to let them affect us.

It is important to emphasize the mutuality of our relationship. We both want it to be the way it is. It takes two partners cooperating with each other to make a marriage work; one can't do it alone. Hester could do her utmost to perceive me positively, but that in itself wouldn't keep us together and happy if I constantly criticized her, ran around with other women, drank to excess, and in general treated her shabbily. Eventually she'd realize that she couldn't meet her love-need through me, and she'd stop trying.

After more than thirty years of marriage, I still find myself struggling with the problem of perceiving my wife positively *regardless of what she does*. This, I believe, is the secret of the saints. Unlocking it requires unremitting effort and dedication. Critical to the success of this endeavor is the ability to *look for those behaviors in our partners that either reinforce our existing positive perceptions or change our negative perceptions to positive ones*. Admittedly, this can sometimes be like searching for the proverbial needle in the haystack. When two people are in the habit of behaving badly toward each other, it can be difficult to sift through the criticism, shouting, and sulking to find the few loving actions that afford a ray of hope. In most marriages, however, they are there *somewhere*. Once we manage to locate them, our behaviors will begin to reflect and reinforce our positive perceptions. And this is the cornerstone upon which a marriage can be rebuilt. Our negative programmed behaviors will slowly be replaced by new behaviors that strengthen our relationships. Those behaviors, in other words, are just programmed; we can change them if we are willing to work at changing our perceptions.

Permanent Love outlines various behaviors couples can cultivate to create lasting relationships. They are effective precisely because they are instrumental in changing people's perceptions of each other. Our perceptions are lodged in our minds, but merely *thinking* them into changing is difficult. *Doing* things will cause them to change more effectively. With thinking alone, fantasies are easily created and believed. Day-to-day activities are rooted in experience and are less likely to be misunderstood. The old saying "what you do speaks so loudly I can't hear what you're saying" seems more appropriate than ever. Doing involves more of ourself than thinking or talking and thus is more effective.

One reason why shared activities are so critical is that they make a couple more aware of each other. For example, you can hardly play racquetball with someone without being aware of what your partner is doing, or you're apt to get brained by the ball. Another reason why shared activities are mandatory for keeping a marriage intact is that they force a couple to interact. If that interaction is pleasant—if you come away from your racquetball game with a good perception of yourself and your partner—this will further enrich your already existing *positive perception* out of which *positive behaviors* will flow.

Shared activities also help a couple get to know each other better. Many of the couples I have counseled over the years have expressed the desire to "really know" their spouses. Most have the notion that "really knowing" means having heart-to-heart conversations about feelings—preferably by candlelight or beside an open fire with soft music playing in the background. But can talking about feelings, even deep and secret ones, fully reveal one person to another? I think not. I believe we reveal ourselves by what we do. Our actions, far better than our words, reflect our wants and our perceptions and who we are. They also reflect whatever disparities may exist between our wants and needs. When I perceive Hester as someone I love and care about, my actions and my behaviors toward her make this clear. The same holds true when I perceive her as not quite the person I want her to be.

Finally, shared activities result in a shared sense of accomplishment, a mutual satisfaction that is one of the strongest positive perceptions to be found. Achieving a goal together, no matter how miniscule it may seem, can work wonders. Whenever Hester and I play cards together, or dance, or take a walk, or do the dishes, or engage in any activity side-by-side, we are strengthening the fabric of our marriage. We are strengthening the lasting positive perception we have of each other and making whatever we are doing that much more enjoyable.

Genuine enjoyment results from *active*, not passive, behavior. If you really want to enjoy something, you first have to be willing to put some effort into it. If I sit back and watch Hester prepare our dinner, I'll enjoy myself less than I will if I work beside her with equal enthusiasm. Also, such passive behaviors such as watching a movie, play, or sporting event have no strengthening quality. The key is that the activity should involve *active participation*, not passive reception.

Obviously, there are some activities we all can and want to do on our own. But doing things alone will not satisfy our love-need. In the process of sharing effortful activities with our partners, we create a couple-confidence that is very different from individual confidence and faith in one's own abilities.

Recently I have watched two small businesses form within my own family. My son Nelson decided to open his own gunsmithing shop after spending nineteen months in gunsmith school. Hester and our oldest daughter, Dorothy, went into the poster business together last year. (My son Thomas joined them recently.) Both ventures required a great deal of self-confidence on the part of everyone involved. As it turned out, Nelson had a much harder time with his business than Hester and Dorothy had with theirs. Part of the problem lay in the fact that he was on his own. Whenever a difficulty arose, he had to handle it by himself. Hester and Dorothy, on the other hand, had each other. They could consult freely and think in tandem about how to approach each day. Nelson satisifed his need to be in control of his life; Hester and Dorothy not only achieved that but were also able to meet their needs for love and belonging.

I cannot overemphasize the importance of doing things alone together, of approaching tasks in harmony and accomplishing them jointly, of taking time daily just to *be alone together*. The biggest mistake most couples make once their children arrive is to neglect spending time together *without the children present*. They get so involved in the day-to-day concerns of running their families and nurturing their children that they forget to nurture each other. Before they know it, they are strangers.

I believe that it is impossible for two people to form a lasting bond unless they set aside a part of every day (or nearly every day) solely for each other. To escape the noise and distractions of our busy household, Hester and I take regular walks together, in the mornings or evenings, depending on our schedules; we usually manage to do this six or seven times a week. And we periodically take brief two- to four-day vacations. We travel to Sedona, a small town in northern Arizona, and stay at a motel where there are no telephones or televisions in the rooms. There we hike along the riverbed or through the dry canyon gulches where the water sometimes flows from the winter snows and rains. These times belong to us alone. They enable us to see the flowers, to see each other, to renew our intimacy.

Whenever there are other people involved, the relationship-strengthening effects of a shared activity are somewhat reduced and the sense of cooperation is diluted. It's nice to spend an occasional evening with another couple, but that does little to reinforce the you-and-I consciousness that is so necessary to closeness and the satisfaction of the love-need. If Hester and I invite another couple over to fix dinner with us, we would all have a good time, but it's just not the same as when Hester and I fix dinner alone together. This doesn't mean that in order to have a healthy relationship a husband and wife must cling together to the exclusion of everyone else and the surrounding world; quite the contrary. We are in and of the world, and we can't shut it out, nor should we try. But we must make room for moments and hours and even days when we only have eyes and ears for each other. I recommend, as a *bare minimum*, one hour a day, three days a week or a half hour together on a daily basis. It's amazing how much these brief periods of time together can satisfy our love-need.

Any relationship demands time and effort: time away from our self-satisfying little pursuits, and the effort to get up off our behinds and pay attention to someone else. Committing ourselves to giving freely of our time and effort, however, is invariably worth it. Developing the habit of spending quality time with our loved ones can change our whole outlook on life. It can be the sole contributing factor to the development of positive perceptions of those persons we most want to be close to.

All marriages have problems, and these problems are remarkably similar from one marriage to the next. No couple has a monopoly on financial difficulties, sexual awkwardness, misbehaving kids, troublesome in-laws, or any of the myriad other conflicts that color our lives. Why, then, do some couples make it while others fail? I don't believe that a happily married couple is any smarter than a miserable one. I do believe that couples who get along together, year after year and crisis after crisis, have something that other couples lack. They hold among themselves the secret of coping with problems as they arise. They have made continuous positive perceptions and behaviors integral to the fabric of their marriage.

Most of the couples I have counseled during my career have come to me with little or no understanding of what it takes to make a relationship work. They have gone into marriage with behaviors learned from their parents and have formed new behaviors of their own without giving much thought to whether these behaviors really satisfy their needs or the needs of their partners. And often they have formed illusions of love that have little to do with what loving is all about.

4

The illusions of love

Back in the mid-sixties, when I was teaching high school, a young girl I had been counseling approached me in the hall between classes. She was clearly upset.

"Look at what he gave me, Mr. Ford," she said, holding out her wrist. On it was a brand-new watch.

"That's a pretty nice watch, Linda," I replied. "Who's the he that gave it to you?"

"My father," she answered. "Who else?"

"Seems like a great gift to me," I went on, hoping to boost her spirits a little.

"But you don't understand," she said plaintively. "This is the fourth watch he's given me. I don't want another watch. I want my father!" Then she burst into tears.

It wasn't until many years later that I fully understood what Linda had been trying to tell me. The situation between her and her father had been tragic—and, as I've since learned, very typical.

We all have wants we believe will satisfy our human needs. We spend our lives pursuing these wants, and when we get them—provided we know what to do with them—we are happy. Often, however, we can't discriminate between genuine wants, or those that we can use to really satisfy our needs, and fantasy wants that only seem to. We may experience a measure of satisfaction from achieving our fantasy wants, but the pleasure never lasts because *it has no roots in any need satisfaction.*

To compound the problem, we assume that our fantasy wants are held in common by the persons around us. So we translate those wants into behaviors. Linda's father apparently believed that receiving gifts met one of his human needs: Caught up in his fantasy, he thought

-51-

that giving gifts was the best way to meet the needs of the persons he loved, including his daughter.

We Americans are great gift-givers. We have several holidays each year on which handing out presents is almost mandatory: Christmas, Mother's Day, Father's Day, Valentine's Day, and now even Grandparents' Day. We give gifts to celebrate and commemorate an assortment of occasions: graduations, birthdays, weddings, anniversaries, promotions, and on and on. We view these gifts as signs of our love—which, in fact, they very well may be. Unfortunately, we also imbue them with fantasy powers. We believe that gifts can not only stand as symbols of our love but also satisfy or even create love. In this we are mistaken.

Don't get me wrong; I'm not averse to gift-giving. When a close, loving relationship already exists between two persons, a gift can reflect or enhance it. Without that preexisting relationship, though, a gift is worthless. It has no inherent qualities of its own. It can't satify love in a vacuum, and it can't effectively manipulate one person into behaving in a loving way toward another. Any such perception of another's action that does arise is in itself a fantasy.

The real problem with giving gifts is that it's frequently the lazy way out. It requires far less energy to simply hand someone a package than it does to spend quality time with him or her. Even when a gift signals our intention to love or an ongoing love, it's meaningless if it isn't accompanied by or followed by quality time spent alone together.

The belief that a gift can satisfy a love-need is one of the many illusions of love. There are countless others. One in particular that is widely held, especially among the young, is the feeling of intense excitement that accompanies meeting someone new. We encounter someone at school, at work, at a party; we're attracted to that person, and instantly we're "in love."

* * *

Martha was a junior in high school and had already had two sexual relationships by the time she came to see me.

Martha's parents had been divorced for three years, and she had seen little of her father since then. He had moved to another state. Her mother had an on-again, off-again live-in romance going with a man Martha "couldn't stand." I learned all of this in our first session together, during which Martha was very outgoing and talkative.

Later, Martha began to open up about what was important to her and what she wanted.

"I'm pretty confused about guys and what they want from me," she admitted. "I felt real close to the last two guys I went with. At first they'd pay a lot of attention to me and we'd talk a lot. But after a while they acted like they didn't care about me. Both times, I ended up feeling used."

"What about sex?" I asked her.

"To me, sex is just something you do. I don't think it's all that great. The guys always want it, though."

She told me that she had "fallen in love" with her first boyfriend long before he'd shown any signs of responding to her. Then, when he had, she'd been tremendously excited.

"He started noticing me, and then he asked me out. I was in heaven! We went together, and we went to bed together, and then it all fell apart. I really wanted to be happy with him, but my feelings just faded away. I guess his did, too."

She paused before going on.

"You know," she finally said, "getting through high school takes a lot of acting. And it can be very lonely at times."

"And what's the best way to get over that loneliness?" I asked.

"I guess it's finding someone you like and who likes you and doesn't get tired of you." Then she began to smile and added, "I guess I'm talking about my mother."

Over the next few months, Martha turned her attention to improving her relationship with her mother. With that love-need on its way to being satisfied, she became far more careful in her choice of "guys" and was able to make more reasoned decisions about her behavior toward them.

* * *

The excitement one feels in the early days of a relationship is not confined to teenagers. Many years ago, a divorced man I had been counseling for quite some time met a woman to whom he was strongly attracted. The attraction was mutual, and before long they were making plans to get married. One day he described to me how thrilling it was to go through the "getting-to-know-someone" stage. "Good Lord, Ed, the excitement of getting close—especially sexually—is sure great," he said. And then he added, somewhat sadly, "But I know it won't last, though it's wonderful now."

Why can't the excitement last? The same reason the excitement of anything new we acquire doesn't last. Once you *have* something, the newness goes and so does the resulting excitement. With humans, though, we have the added dimension of love-need satisfaction that picks up where the excitement or the newness of the relationship leaves off. Most couples settle into a sort of boredom with each other. They stop perceiving each other as exciting, as someone they *want* to do something with or for. They assume that, once married, their needs are met. They replace their active *wanting* perceptions (and behaviors) with passive *having* ones. And the behaviors that have been programmed to flow from those perceptions change.

The people who tend to become most enthralled by the exciting illusion of love are those who attempt to escape unhappy marriages by having affairs. The exhilaration of meeting a lover in an out-of-the-way place; of seeing the person waiting for you impatiently; of thinking back to stolen moments and ahead to still more; the long talks and ready intimacy—all of these can combine to create quite an illusion of a strong relationship when, in fact, it's built on sand. Regardless of how intense an affair of this type can be, it rarely if ever satisfies the love-need. And the intensity never lasts.

We create fantasy wants and engage in those behaviors we believe will "work" to help us get our fantasy wants. We fool ourselves into thinking we're happy when our happiness in itself is an illusion. In the midst of our self-deception, though, our brains know what's going on. No matter how hard we try, we can't fool our brains. We may eat junk food in an attempt to satisfy our food-need, but sooner or later our brains will warn us of the damage we're doing to our bodies. The same is true for love. We may structure an entire marriage around illusions, but one day our brains will reveal to us the well of loneliness we're trapped in.

How, then, can we go about satisfying our love-need in a true and lasting way? We have to control our perceptions and program our behaviors to conform to and reinforce the wants that will satisfy our needs. Recall that we aren't born with behaviors; we have to *learn* them. And we learn them initially from our parents and others who raised us and taught us when we were young.

When I married Hester, I brought into our marriage certain ideas about love I'd gotten from my parents, teachers, babysitters, camp counselors, and others I'd come into contact with during my growing years. I had courted Hester according to the custom of the times, and my behavior throughout our courtship had reflected traditional ways of thinking.

We soon settled into a routine of living that reflected what we had learned from our culture and especially from our parents. Neither of us had given any thought to what "made" a marriage work, nor had we given any thought to working at our marriage. To both of us, marriage was the natural result of meeting someone you were attracted to and following the urge to get married. Our perceptions were echoed by those around us; when I began dating Hester, her father told her, "That boy is ready to get married." By that he meant that since I had finished school and had a job, the next step in my development was bound to be marriage, followed by the raising of a family. This made sense. It was the way people lived their lives. I had no desire to "have my own place" or "my own life" or to just live with a woman and then "split when we got tired of each other." None of those options fell within my frame of reference.

Also, it never occurred to me to try to make my marriage the best it could be. I didn't think about what to do; I simply did whatever entered my mind at the time. On the evening of our first day at home together following our honeymoon, Hester made dinner. After we had finished eating, I got up, left the kitchen, and went into the living room to read the newspaper while Hester did the dishes. That was the way things had been done in both of our homes while we were growing up; why should we do anything differently? When we went out, it was generally in the company of other couples, and we attended many parties. We engaged in very few activities alone together—not because we didn't want to, but because the importance of doing things alone together never occurred to us. The idea that effortful shared activities can make a marriage better didn't strike me until almost twenty-five years *after* we married.

The affection Hester and I showed each other followed closely the models we'd seen in our own homes. In Hester's family, physical affection had rarely been demonstrated toward the children after childhood and almost never by her parents toward each other. My own parents had been somewhat more demonstrative, so I tended to be more openly affectionate than she. This is not to say that I was better than Hester in this regard, or that she was cold or uncaring; we just behaved differently. I remember, once our children started coming along, how I used to watch with some degree of envy as she showered the babies with affection—as her mother had done before her. We were both the products of what we had learned during our upbringings, and our behaviors toward each other and our children reflected what we had experienced long before we met. In time, we changed some of those behaviors or replaced them with others. But we had to *learn* those new behaviors, as we had learned the old ones.

Getting married today bears a strong resemblance to what it was like nearly thirty years ago. Things haven't changed that much, if at all. Couples still bring into marriage whatever they learned while they were growing up. If their own parents were loving and supportive, then they have some idea of what it takes to be loving and supportive to their partners. If they weren't, however, they have little or nothing to draw on when it comes time to make their own marriages work.

Unfortunately, we seem to learn negative behaviors far more readily than we learn positive ones. Most couples learn all about how to fight. Many learn how to separate and, if they don't manage to reconcile with each other, how to divorce. Very few learn how to get along. In this, we tend to have inadequate teachers, who themselves have learned from other inadequate teachers, and so on back through generations. We enter into our relationships having learned old behaviors, and when these don't have the desired effect of making us happy, we rarely think about where to turn. In the past, it seems, people were more willing to grit their teeth and suffer. I believe that one reason for today's high divorce rate is the fact that couples are less inclined to put up with what their parents endured.

Couple after couple come to me laden with behaviors they've learned and can't seem to shake. Some already have divorced two or three times and are desperate to make their present marriages last. I see many marriages in which both partners work and neither has any idea of what to do with the other when alone at home. Their time together usually consists of following individual or solitary pursuits. One watches television while the other reads; one goes out to a spa while the other does the housework; one cooks dinner while the other walks the dog; one visits his or her parents while the other retreats into a hobby or special project. To them, marriage means coexisting under the same roof. They assume that they'll stay together until something comes along to "cause" the breakup of their relationship. They live each day as if they were at the mercy of "outside forces" that could drive them apart at any moment. And when they do experience money problems, or sex problems, or in-law problems, or when one starts nagging or the other starts staying late at the office, they point the finger of blame at the supposed "cause" of their unhappiness. They forget that everyone has problems and that no marriage is immune to them. The happy couples who stay together because they want to, year after year, are those whose love-needs are being continually fulfilled. That feeling of satisfaction and happiness has given them both the willingness and the ability to solve their problems as they arise.

I've also seen couples who sincerely believe that their marriages are going well when things are falling to pieces in every other area of their lives. They don't see the connection between the lack of real love-need fulfillment in their marriage and, for example, their job or physical ailments. And this is yet another illusion of love.

* * *

Jake was a thirty-one-year-old salesman for a power transmission equipment firm. He had been married to Patty for seven years. They had two children: Sue, who was four, and John, who was nearly two.

About three years before we met, Jake had begun developing health problems. By the time he walked into my office, he was a wreck. He was having constant chest pains, his heart would suddenly begin accelerating for no reason, and he was unable to sleep. He was at the point where he could no longer go to work. He'd get into his car, break out in a cold sweat, start shaking, and eventually give up and return to the house.

Jake had already seen several doctors, none of whom had found anything wrong with him. His heart and chest had been checked repeatedly. Finally, his family physician had suggested he make an appointment with a psychiatrist. The psychiatrist in turn had recommended that Jake spend eight weeks in a hospital psychiatric unit, away from his family and job. Jake couldn't stand the thought of being separated from Patty for so long; as a sort of last-ditch effort to stave off a decision he thought was inevitable, he came to me.

During our first session, Jake recounted the progressive development of his symptoms. I then asked him to describe for me what he did both at home and on the job.

"I spend most of my day calling on accounts," he said. "Then I go back to the office to put the orders together. Sometimes I work twelve to fourteen hours a day, six days a week."

"Do you like your work?" I asked.

"I love it! I've been with the same company for five years now. That's why I'm so scared of messing things up. I don't want to lose my job."

"Are you in danger of losing it?"

"When I first started getting sick, I wasn't—or so my boss said. He'd had some health problems himself about ten years earlier and had worked things out. He told me not to worry because I was the best salesman he had. Now, though, I'm not sure. How can I keep my job if I can't even get to work?"

"What about your family? How are things going with them?"

"Just fine, considering the way I feel. I'm close to my children, but I'm closest to Patty. We've always gotten along and have very few disagreements or arguments."

"What do you do together?"

"Not a whole lot, I'm afraid," he confessed. "There just isn't time. I get home pretty late and don't see much of the kids—but they're still a little young for me to enjoy. I'm sure that will change."

"What do you and Patty do?" I asked.

"Well, by the time I come home she and the kids have usually eaten. She leaves dinner in the oven for me. I sort of gulp it down—I've always been a fast eater—and take my dishes to the sink. Then I go into the living room and relax by reading the paper and watching TV. After putting Sue and John to bed, Patty usually joins me there."

A familiar pattern was beginning to emerge. The more we talked, the more I understood Jake's problem.

He and Patty spent most of their weekends visiting their parents and had an occasional evening out in the company of friends. The two of them had not been away from home together for three years, since Jake had won a sales contest and a free trip.

Although Jake had played many sports when he was younger, he hadn't carried any of those interests into his adult life. He didn't exercise and wasn't involved in any kind of physical activity. For a while he had taken up stamp collecting, but his interest in that, too, had passed.

What I saw was a well-meaning, highly energetic man who loved his family, liked his job—and satisfied absolutely none of his human needs at home. His life away from work was totally devoid of those activities that are essential to fulfilling human needs. He did nothing alone with Patty, nothing with his children, and nothing for himself that met his needs for love and belonging, for getting along with his family and enjoying being with them. The lack of need-fulfillment, I was convinced, was the reason behind his failing health.

I worked with him to develop a plan to improve his home life. At first, he was puzzled. "I thought you were way off when I left your office that first day," he told me months later. When he considered the alternative his psychiatrist had recommended, he decided to continue working with me.

Since Jake felt closer to Patty than to either of his children, we made a plan for him to start spending some quality alone time by doing a jigsaw puzzle with her on a daily basis. Gradually we introduced other activities— washing the dishes together, playing card games, working in the yard. Then I focused on getting Jake together individually with Sue and John. He began playing with each of them alone, sometimes taking them for walks or playing a game.

After having a complete physical, Jake embarked on an exercise program that ultimately turned into a daily bike ride—at first alone, and later, if time permitted, with his son John buckled into an infant seat on the back.

Before long, Jake was sleeping soundly at night. The more he worked at integrating himself with his family in need-fulfilling activities, the more his symptoms receded. He returned to work half-days and finally full time. Rather than rushing through lunch or skipping it altogether, he took walks during his lunch hour. Within four months, his health problems had disappeared.

Once I called Patty to confirm Jake's next appointment. I asked her how things were going, and she reflected for a moment before replying.

"I thought we had a great marriage before this all happened," she said. "But now, after getting into the habit of doing things with Jake, I realized how dull it was."

Their fantasy of what a marriage should be had been replaced by a new and positive reality. From that point on, they took time each week to review everything they'd done together and plan new activities to share alone with each other as well as with the children.

At our last session, Jake bounded in, happy and fit, to exclaim, "Patty's decided that she's never going to be happy with the way our marriage is. She's going to keep looking for ways to make it even better!"

* * *

This case was especially interesting to me because it proved something I'd suspected for quite some time: namely, that symptoms—and feelings—are merely masks for what we are doing or not doing. Often, therapists see only the masks their clients are wearing without ever getting behind them to the source of the problem: the lack of human need-fulfillment.

Many people come to me wearing masks of depression, anger, guilt, or, as Jake demonstrated, physical pain. They have the preconceived notion that counseling involves talking about whatever is "preventing" them from enjoying their lives. They think that bringing their past, or thoughts, or feelings out into the open willl make their problems more manageable or even make them disappear.

I do not believe that talking about problems can "cure" an unhappy marriage. Whenever I begin a counseling relationship with a couple, I start with a few moments of casual conversation to ease the tension. Then I move immediately to questions designed to find out whether or not they really want to work at their marriage. I find out if they are willing to make a mutual commitment to cooperate with one another in the weeks and months ahead to make their marriage better. If they (one or both) are not willing to work at it, they don't need me, they need a lawyer. If they want to work at the marriage, I then try and ascertain two things: what they're doing at the time to satisfy their love-need through each other and what they could do that they are not doing that would help.

This is seldom what they expect. So I frequently find myself in a conversation like the following: "It all started back when he (she) began..." or "I guess our biggest problem is money (or sex, kids or whatever)…" or "And if only he (she) would stop…" or "We want to tell you about our problems."

"Has talking about your problems helped you in the past?" I ask.

"No," they reply, "but it helps to understand why we feel the way we do."

"Does understanding why you feel the way you do help the two of you to get along better?" I persist. "Does it make you any happier?"

"No," they admit, "but aren't we supposed to talk about our problems and feelings?"

"Not here," I say with a smile. "If I spent all day listening to other persons' problems, I'd get depressed, and that's not something I'm willing to put myself through."

"Then what *can* we talk about?" they want to know.

"How about discussing what you can do, both together and individually, to build strength and confidence in each other and improve your marriage?" I suggest. "You already know how to make things worse. Let's work together to learn how to make them better."

It's no wonder that couples have so many illusions about what marriage is and how relationships are built and rebuilt. The media are full of people who talk endlessly about the importance of "getting in touch with their feelings." Go into any bookstore today, and you'll find countless "self-help" books that stress that point. Few if any even mention the fact that a marriage is something that takes work, lots of work, by two people who are committed to seeing it through and learning what it takes to achieve that goal.

One of the most widespread illusions of love is that "communicating" can somehow engender love and keep it alive. Nearly every day, we hear someone babbling on about "open communication," "telling it like it is," "expressing yourself," and "letting people know how you feel." The theory is that the more we talk, the more clearly we'll understand each other and the closer we'll become. In truth, most of us can't understand ourselves, let alone anyone else! And how can "getting to know" someone else teach us how to deal more effectively with our problems? I don't think it can. As a matter of policy, I am totally against having my clients talk things over *unless they are sufficiently strong as a couple to do so.* Otherwise, long conversations become a sort of petri dish for all kinds of new and virulent bugs. Each person tries to manipulate the other into believing or doing something. The person with the stronger verbal skills usually emerges as the victor. And what does that prove? Nothing. Even worse, a couple may come away from a particularly long and emotional conversation with the illusion that things have gotten better. Of course, they haven't. But the problems that do exist in the marriage that are the symptoms of its breakdown will have been buried beneath the weight of words.

When I agree to see two persons whose relationship is troubled, I insist at the outset that they not talk about their problems. No "headtripping" allowed! In a weak marriage, unfettered talking can easily degenerate into fighting. Even in a strong marriage, conversation has to be handled carefully. Talking can be used as an excuse to avoid action. Often, couples will have a long talk lasting into the early hours of the morning. They then go to bed, satisfied that their problems have been resolved. Unless the talk is accompanied by a positive change in their mutual pattern of behavior, they have only created another illusion.

Interestingly, once a couple has formed the habit of spending quality time alone together and their marriage has grown stronger, talking becomes less essential and more natural. They begin to enjoy themselves and each other without having the need to explain or verbally dissect everything about their relationship. They maintain a steady, comfortable stream of conversation rather than setting aside times for "talking things out"—times that formerly proved traumatic or destructive.

Yet another illusion of love is the assumption that two people will automatically have identical expectations and perceptions of their relationship simply because they've agreed to have a relationship. Ancient Greek mythology tells of three women who shared the same eye; I have yet to meet a couple who shares the same brain! Some couples have radically differing wants or perceptions while demonstrating very similar behaviors. When those wants and perceptions are finally revealed, the effects can be devastating.

* * *

Helen was a single parent with two children, ages eight and six. She had been divorced for two years. When I met her, she had been living for a year with Bob, a foreman in the manufacturing plant where she was employed.

Over the past few months, Helen's behavior at work had grown increasingly erratic. She forgot to do jobs she was assigned and had started calling in sick, complaining of migraine headaches. She was close to being fired and had agreed to counseling as a condition for being kept on. She also knew she was in trouble and wanted help.

Helen was a quiet person with few close friends. Bob filled a great void for her. Unfortunately, her perception of their relationship was quite different from his. Helen had created an elaborate fantasy perception of how things were between them; to her, how they were living and acting toward each other signaled the presence of true love, and she was convinced that they would get married sooner or later. Bob, on the other hand, perceived their living arrangement from another perspective entirely. He had already been married and divorced twice, and although he liked sharing a home with Helen, he had no intention of marrying her.

Helen was deeply wounded when she learned what Bob had intended. The difference between what she wanted (Bob to marry her) and what she suddenly perceived (Bob's refusal to do anything of the kind) caused a major perceptual difference or stress in her brain. What she chose to do—erratic behavior—was soon all too evident on her job.

"And I thought he really loved me!" she told me tearfully. "How can he say he loves me—and act as if he loves me—and then turn around and tell me that he'll never marry me? I don't understand!"

* * *

Helen's predicament raised a number of questions in my mind. Can two persons express genuine love for each other just by moving in together, or must they marry to make this expression valid? How does this affect how each person perceives the relationship? Can existing together under the same roof bind a couple as strongly as the marriage vows? The more I thought about it, the more I became convinced that Helen wasn't the only one who had a fantasy perception of the way things were between her and Bob. He did, too. And what was his fantasy perception? That his "love" for Helen was genuine when it was devoid of the commitment to work at getting along with another that love demands.

I'm not saying that Bob didn't care for Helen; he probably did. But did he really love her? I think not. Perhaps I'm old-fashioned, but I believe that marriage and all it involves—including the promise to continually work at the relationship in good times and bad—is the ultimate in love between two adults. To me, *the commitment that marriage both connotes and requires is what makes the love-need attainable*. The idea that our love-need can be satisfied without that commitment may be the greatest of all illusions of love.

When people come to me insisting that they want to leave their spouse although they still "love" them, I realize that their use of the word "love" is very different from mine. To me, *love is the willingness to work at getting along with another person*; that is the way I defined it in *Permanent Love*, and that is the way I define it today. Love without that degree of commitment to work at the relationship is only a shell, a shadow of what it could be. Living together by its very nature allows for a lesser commitment or none at all. It implies that while you may perceive the other person as someone you want to share a home with, you don't necessarily perceive him or her as someone you think is *worth* working at building a love relationship with—at least you are not yet willing to make a commitment. Even a marriage certificate doesn't carry with it the strong commitment needed for a marriage to last. The perception of *what a commitment means* can vary widely between spouses. For many, marriage commitment may be perceived as "until we get divorced." Giving up and finding someone else can become a substitute for hard work.

This lack of commitment is fine for roommates; it isn't very wise for two persons who expect their relationship to be intimate and involved. Almost invariably, at least one of them begins to hurt. One of them begins fulfilling his or her love-need through the other. And once you achieve some measure of success at satisfying your love-need through another person, it becomes increasingly difficult to pull away and stop loving him or her. In time, you develop an attachment, a dependency, a desire for permanence that can be quite painful to deny.

The human condition seems to be such that once we have found someone whom we can successfully love, we are nourished by the overwhelming satisfaction that brings. We glimpse in that satisfaction something that has eternal merit and is more profound than anything we have ever known. We are lifted out of our daily lives into an experience that transcends life itself. How can we believe that it will not last forever?

The casual relationships that are so popular today reflect the shifting mores of our throwaway society. We value persons at far less than their worth. When we tire of one person, we move out to find someone else. We treat people as we treat cars: We keep the one we have for a few years and trade it in when a newer and more appealing model comes along. It's almost as if we enter into relationships assuming that they'll end. And if this is so, why bother with marriage? Since divorce is such a hassle, why not just obviate the need for it?

Genuine love isn't casual, nor is it temporary. It can't be developed and satisfied over and over again with one friend after another. The death of a child can tear out the heart of a parent. Equally painful can be the separation from someone we love. It involves weathering difficulties and struggles, sharing and solving problems, and establishing a mutual confidence—all of which literally takes years. This isn't true only of love between a couple. I look at my children today, and while I sincerely believe that I have loved each of them from the moment of birth, I now feel closer to them than I ever thought possible. I have a special reverence for them that I label one of the greatest rewards of parenting. None of this happened overnight. The more value we place on a human being, the greater the pain of separation. Love-need fulfillment with a person means *we have bestowed the highest value we can on another.*

When two persons agree to marry, they are accepting (or should be) the responsibility for working at loving each other. I didn't marry Hester simply because I wanted her to love *me* and make *me* happy; rather, I chose her as the person through whom I wanted to fulfill my need for love. Marriage was the means by which I made that known to her and revealed my willingness to work at loving her. It was the external sign of my internal commitment. Loving someone today and abandoning them for someone else tomorrow tears at the very fabric of our love-need satisfaction. The one who is left behind is not the only one who is thrown away.

When Bob told Helen, "Sorry, but I don't want to get tied down again," he was really saying, "I don't want to work at loving you because *you're not worth the risk.*" By refusing to marry Helen, he was in effect assigning to her a *lower value* than he'd assigned to either of his first two wives. Bob had divorced both of them and was now living with her. How could he value her less? Once she learned what he truly wanted to do with her, she experienced enormous turmoil and conflict, and she had to struggle for months to regain her sense of self-worth. Part of her struggle involved leaving behind her fantasy perception of him, her illusion that he loved her in the same way she loved him.

If we listen to what our brains tell us, most of us can ascertain when we're really being loved and when we aren't. When our love-need and worth-need are satisfied, our brains let us know. When it isn't, our brains send out all kinds of warning signals. Children seem more adept at picking up on these signals than adults. For example, they quickly recognize the difference between being loved and being bought off with gifts. The child who is inundated with money and gifts and otherwise ignored by his or her parents is the child who's starved for love and worth.

The satisfaction of our love-need is as basic to our well-being as the satisfaction of our need for nutritional foods. If we persist in eating nothing but empty calories, we may feel as though we've had enough to eat, but our brains will soon sound the alarm.

From what the media are telling us these days, love is every bit as accessible as junk food. And we use the word with about as much seriousness as we buy a hamburger. We "love" our jobs, our clothes, our cars, our furniture; we "love" sailing or skiing; we "love" the latest movie or bestselling book. No wonder couples get married without having the slightest idea of what love is. No wonder they have so little understanding of how much effort it takes to build and maintain a need-satisfying relationship. Their heads are full of illusions. They view love as something that either "exists" between two people or doesn't; as long as it "exists," things will work out and they'll be happy. But when love "goes away," it's time to get a divorce and start looking for someone else. It's almost as if love is a third person in the marriage, someone who can come and go freely without asking anyone else's permission. Too many people today fail to realize that the deep satisfaction of a warm, loving relationship is something *over which they have control.*

It is up to *me* to determine how much I love Hester, and it is up to *her* to determine how much she loves me. It is up to both of us working together to determine the context in which we will love each other. The context we have chosen is our marriage. Within it, we are each responsible for seeing to it that our own love-needs are satisfied. All Hester can do for me is *make herself available as the person through whom I can fulfill my love-need.* The same is all I can do for her. During the first twenty years of our marriage, I honestly didn't know what love involved and the amount of hard work it took to achieve it. Fortunately, Hester was willing to put up with what were, in retrospect, some pretty erratic behaviors on my part. It wasn't until the last decade or so that I realized how many of the things I used to do were merely foolish and misguided attempts to meet my needs.

We all want to be happy. I doubt that anyone could say with a straight face that he or she was totally indifferent to the prospect of happiness (need-fulfillment). We all have human needs, and we spend our lives pursuing those wants which we feel have the best chance of fulfilling those needs. More often than not, we run headlong into blank walls. Either the wants we've been pursuing won't really satisfy our needs, or we don't know what to do with what we want once we have it. Our ideas of the way we *think* things should be collapsed like a house of cards when measured against our need-satisfaction.

When a couple comes to me and asks, "How can we find real happiness?" I say to them: "You must each accept responsibility for yourself, for there is nothing else over which you have control. You must sweep away your illusions of love and begin in earnest to work at loving each other. And once you achieve love, you will see it for what it is: the greatest joy available to men and women on this earth."

5

The illusions of sex

The illusions of love seem pale beside the illusions of sex. Somehow the biological urge or basic need to couple has been transformed by our culture (and others) into a whole array of glittering illusions. Sex is used to sell everything from toothpaste to electric garage door openers. It is used as a tool for manipulating, abusing, and controlling others, for giving and receiving pleasure, for punishing and rewarding. It is held up as a priceless gift and dismissed as a commodity. It can be humiliating or exhilarating, meaningful or meaningless. For some couples, sex is an integral and comfortable part of their relationship; for others, it is something that happens too often or not often enough, or at all of the wrong times and none of the right ones. It is ever-present on stage, screen, and television, in books, magazines, and ads, in conversations. It almost seems to permeate the air we breathe.

Surrounded by sex on all sides, as it were, we frequently find ourselves confused and boggled by what it is and what it isn't. Much of our confusion, I believe, has its source in the complex relationship among sex, affection, and love. Sex *seems* to be closely tied to love and affection, and most people would profess that it in fact is; yet there are those who view sex as something to be enjoyed for its own sake, in the presence or absence of caring. While many people maintain that sex is safe and good and right only within the context of a commitment such as marriage, others claim that they have managed to free sex from the bonds of love and are perfectly happy with the results.

The myriad ways—most of them conflicting—in which we perceive sex were illustrated with great clarity and insight in Blake Edwards' 1979 film, "10." It is the story of a middle-aged man, George Weber (Dudley Moore), who becomes so infatuated with a beautiful woman, Ginny (Bo Derek), that he follows her and her new husband to where they are honeymooning. When her husband falls asleep on his surfboard and begins drifting out to sea, George rescues him. The husband ends up in the hospital, badly sunburned, and George ends up alone with Ginny. The two have dinner together, after which she seduces him to the strains of Ravel's "Bolero." Following their sexual encounter, her husband telephones and Ginny chats with him in George's presence. By this time George has begun feeling guilty, and when Ginny hangs up the phone he asks her how she can be so casual about sleeping with another man while on her honeymoon.

He questions her as to why she got married when a week later she's having an affair with the man who saved her husband's life. Ginny is puzzled by George's concern. Her belief is that if a person "feels" like having sex with someone, married or single, he or she should have it.

George is somewhat frustrated with her casual attitude toward sexual involvement and argues the importance of why one does it and with whom. Finally, still perplexed by George's inability to understand "her world," Ginny says, "I don't know what your problem is, but I don't think you're going to solve it by trying to solve mine. I don't really think I have a problem."

At this point, George delivers what I consider to be the classic line of the movie: "That's your problem."

For me, this scene from "10" typifies many of the most prevalent illusions of sex. George is consumed by his fantasy perception of Ginny; when he finally "gets" her, his fantasy is shattered. Ginny views George merely as someone to have a good time with, and sex as a sort of snack food; for her, sex and love and affection have nothing to do with one another. George is shocked at

Ginny's attitude; Ginny is annoyed by what she considers to be George's old-fashioned ideas.

There are many books and films around today that have at their core the perception of sex Ginny exemplifies. They give sex a life of its own and argue that it's there for anyone who can get it—married or not, committed or not. In *How to Make Love to a Man* (New York: Clarkson Potter, Inc., 1981), for example, Alexandra Penney distinguishes between "making love" and "having sex." When two persons "make love," the author claims,

> Affection and caring are paramount. Making love is not just a matter of reaching physical satisfaction. It also involves two people who are helping each other reach emotional and spiritual fulfillment. When you have made love, there is a feeling of having given and having received. It doesn't matter how and when and who had an orgasm first, because making love is not just a purely physical act. (p. 24)

On the surface, the idea that lovemaking is a vehicle for reaching "emotional and spiritual fulfillment" seems pretty grand. But what do these words really mean? Fulfillment of what—a need? What need? The need for love? Hardly. The need for sex? That seems to be what Penney is saying, but I doubt that's what she means, since she's so careful to separate "making love" from "having sex." And where does this sense of fulfillment come from? On high?

And what about the "feeling of having given and having received"? Is she talking here about people giving and receiving love? I don't think so. Sex? Absolutely. But so what? In mulling over these words, I can't help but think that my perception of "making love" and Penney's are vastly different.

She goes on to define "having sex" as "almost wholly a physical experience with sexual services purchased and performed." Then she states the following concept, and suddenly things aren't that simple anymore:

> Pure physical sex can be perfectly terrific if you are
> with someone you care for, because there is an
> element of mutual fun and pure physical excite-
> ment about it. (p. 24)

Hold on. What's this about "having sex" with "someone
you care for"? Isn't the author admitting here that a
modicum of affection—or even of love—is necessary in
order for sex to be "perfectly terrific"? What happens
when neither affection nor love is present? Is sex then
"perfectly boring"? If this is the case, why bother? What's
to be gained from "sexual services purchased and performed"? Certainly the satisfaction of the sexual urge.
But what does this "sexual satisfaction" do to our *perception* of love and affection, and of our self as well as
the person with whom we are sexually involved? And
what does it do to our attempts to satisfy our need for
love?

It's very easy to confuse sex with love, sex with affection, and affection with love. Before going any further, I want to define what I mean by each.

Love is a human need. To fulfill this need, two persons have to work hard at getting along with each other.
They have to do things for and with each other. When
you truly love someone, you are constantly giving of
yourself and making yourself available to the other person as someone through whom he or she can satisfy his
or her love-need—and the other person is doing the
same for you. Simply getting to know a person, growing
fond of him or her, or feeling attracted to another isn't
the same as loving the person. Love takes time and
effort. It never simply "happens." That's why the idea
of "falling in love" is an illusion.

What we think of as "falling in love" is actually little
more than a strong attraction to another or a desire to
be with him or her. Nature has endowed us all with the

tendency to be physically, emotionally, and socially attracted to certain others. When our attraction is reciprocated (and sometimes even when it isn't), we experience intense feelings that are heightened by the newness and thrill of discovery. There's nothing wrong with these feelings; in fact, they can set the stage for real love to grow. There *is* something wrong, however, with believing that they're what love is all about.

"Falling in love" and "staying in love" are radically different from each other. At best, "falling in love" is a beginning, a transition between initially feeling strong attraction and later learning what to do to create the feeling that comes from love-need satisfaction. Most happy couples who have been married for many years (thirty-two for me) look back now and realize that what we at first thought was love was only a hint of what lay in store for us. For those of us who have struggled to stay in love and evinced a perpetual willingness to work at it, love is far more than we ever could have hoped it would be. It's seldom accompanied by the sound of trumpets or a display of fireworks. It's hardly ever found in cozy candlelit restaurant corners or on romantic Caribbean cruises or in the midst of intense discussions. Instead, its presence is felt most acutely in the kitchen, bathroom, or family room, around crying kids and a ringing phone and a dinner burned on the stove.

The miracle of a genuine love relationship is that it doesn't stop at just fulfilling our love-need. *It fulfills all our other human needs as well.* When we are with someone who is continually thinking of ways to fulfill their need for love through us, doing things for and with us, and making it clear that he or she wants to be in our presence, we can't help but feel a sense of self-worth. The more we engage in enjoyable activities together, the more our need for enjoyment is met. When our partner brings us into his or her life and circle of friends, our need for belonging is met. When we are happy and content in a love relationship and things seem to be going the way we want them to, our need for control is met. In other words, the experience of loving and being loved over-flows within us and touches all parts of our lives.

Although I wouldn't term affection a human need, it can be an important sign of love. When we hold, touch, kiss, or embrace a person, we are demonstrating through these behaviors how we perceive another and that we want him or her in our world. There are other shows of affection that are not physical: For example, a smile, a pleasant "Good morning," saying "Thanks" or "I'm glad you're here" or "It's nice to see you"—all of these may be construed as indications of caring. So may laugh-ing at a loved one's jokes, bringing flowers or a thought-ful gift, doing special favors for him or her—the list goes on and on.

Our understanding of the intent and value of affection is with us from birth. Most of the things we do have to be learned, but there are few of us who do not know how to accept and enjoy affection immediately. When our parents held and caressed us, they were showing us the good, uninhibited, spontaneous nature of affec-tion that stems from love. Unfortunately, this easy out-pouring of affection stops in many families once the children have passed through infancy. Too many chil-dren grow up believing that affection should be limited to the very young, when it may be even more desper-ately needed during the late childhood and teen years.

In general, affection is evidence of respect or a sense of value that already exists. This recognition may not always be love, however. In some cultures, a show of affection indicates a respect for another; for example, European men commonly greet one another by kissing. Some people are affectionate toward nearly everyone they meet. Through kind words and friendly hand-shakes, they are demonstrating a general care and con-cern for others. Affection can also be manipulative. Salespeople are taught to make their prospects more comfortable and receptive by shaking their hands heart-ily, putting an arm around a shoulder, or patting the person's back. Often, this "sales" approach is used during courtship; more than one person has been deceived by an overly affectionate lover who almost instantly reverted to rather cold and unaffectionate ways following marriage.

And, of course, affection can be a prelude and an accompaniment to a sexual encounter. This is where major misunderstandings can occur. When one person is attentive, gentle, thoughtful, and kind to another on the way to and in bed, does this mean that love is present? Not necessarily—and perhaps not at all. What's more important is how the person behaves during other times and whether he or she evidences the desire to work at getting along on a regular basis. In situations in which the excitement level is high, it's tempting to confuse affection with love. This is a problem many adolescents have, especially if they have not been shown affection consistently through their growing-up years. They meet someone they're attracted to, that person responds, and instantly the two assume they're in love. Their expectations of what that means can fall on opposite ends of the perceptual spectrum, though. I once counseled a high-school senior who broke up with his girlfriend because she wanted to "make out" and he didn't.

It's also tempting to confuse affection with sexual overtures; affection isn't always a prelude to sex, even in bed. I've counseled a number of persons over the years who have admitted that they were reluctant to show affection to their spouses in bed for fear that it would lead to unwanted sexual episodes. Most frequently, this happens with couples who have never formed the habit of being affectionate on a day-to-day basis. In their experience, a hug in bed always leads to sex; if they don't want sex, they forgo the hug. And that's too bad.

Sex, like love, is a need. Through it, we keep our species alive. It is not basic to keeping ourselves as individuals alive, however; many people, whether by choice or by chance, live totally without sex and do just fine.

And the basic need for sex is not the same as the human need for love. Basically, the need for sex has to do with our bodies' internal functions—like the needs for food and water. The human need for love, on the other hand, has to do with how we deal with the external world.

In the early stages of human development, sex and love were tied more closely than they seem to be today. This was largely due to the fact that both parents were essential to the survival of a child. They found that staying together and working cooperatively for the sake of the child's growth and development until it grew old enough and strong enough to face the world on its own had another payoff. As the parents learned to get along with each other, they also learned how much more pleasant it was to face the trials of life with someone else than to go it alone. Staying together began to be perceived as not only beneficial to the child but also as a highly satisfying way to fulfill all of their human needs. And the intimate loving relationship had another great advantage: continual sexual pleasure with the same person. Our modern definition of love—as the satisfaction that comes from living happily and continually with another person—is probably not all that different from the way our ancestors saw it.

The need for love, then, may be said to have grown out of the need for sex, which has at its root the need to keep our species going. But sex brings with it an intense pleasure that has always appealed to humans, whether or not the intent to have children was present and acknowledged. Prior to the widespread availability of birth control, the distinct possibility of conceiving went hand-in-hand with the pursuit of that pleasure. So people had to make the effort to connect sex with committed love. It is no longer necessary—biologically speaking, at least, or even culturally speaking—to establish that connection, and this has occasioned a whole host of problems.

Most of us still want to perceive sex and love as closely related. This makes us susceptible to one of *the greatest illusions of sex: that it somehow creates an intimacy that will prove to be longstanding.* This in turn leads us to view sex as a vehicle for making and maintaining relationships— and we are disappointed again and again as each relationship we begin in that way disintegrates. Or we use sex to mask the feelings of loneliness we have when our love-need is unfulfilled, never stopping to realize that a series of sexual encounters will do nothing but further frustrate that need. Or we get so caught up in the pleasures of sex that we forget to work at getting along with our partner at other times. A purely sexual relationship gets old very quickly; if sex is all that binds two persons together, they will invariably drift apart. Novelty cannot sustain itself.

Because of the prevalence of birth-control devices, and because of changing cultural mores concerning sex (which, incidentally, seem to be changing back again), we have had the freedom to explore and experiment with sex. We talk about it far less self-consciously than our parents did. In general, we are less embarrassed by it, which is all to the good. But, as many people have found, it is easy to take this freedom too far. Recreational sex, group sex, sex with strangers—these can't begin to satisfy the human needs for love and belonging.

Some people use sex almost like a drug. The euphoric feelings created during a sexual encounter conceal the absence of those feelings which reflect the love-need fulfillment. Once the deed is done, as it were, and the pleasure has subsided, there is nothing left. Many of the people I have worked with have told me how painful it is to come crashing down from a sexual high. One man, a recovering alcoholic, confessed to me that he had been "going through women" in much the same way he used to go through liquor. "After I get out of bed," he said, his eyes filling with tears, "I feel so empty. I look at the woman still in bed, and I realize that there's nothing there—no love, no affection, nothing."

We place great importance on sexual prowess and technique. Countless books have come out in recent years detailing the whys and wherefores of deriving the maximum amount of enjoyment from sex. Countless therapists are now making their livings telling people how to enjoy sex; in a way, I find it amusing that an entire profession has formed around the need to instruct people in an act that human beings have been performing since day one. I have nothing against teaching couples the basics of taking and giving pleasure through sex; in fact, I am all for it. But I question the attempt by some to remove sex from its proper perspective and elevate it to a position of importance where it simply doesn't belong.

I believe that couples should learn everything they can about sex, since this should make their sex lives together more enjoyable. I also believe that couples should learn everything they can about food preparation, since this should make their meals together more enjoyable. In both instances, it helps if you know what you're doing. But neither activity should be seen as the hub around which your relationship revolves. Neither has much of anything to do with the rest of the time you spend together.

When Hester and I were first married, we took dance lessons that have since made the hours we've spent dancing far more pleasurable. Over the years, we've learned to do other things, too—such as playing tennis or studying art together. And we've also learned to give and receive pleasure through sex. Had we depended totally on dancing, or tennis, or art, or sex to keep us together, however, we would have been in trouble. For a marriage to survive, it must consist of a series of shared activities, each contributing to the relationship and ensuring its continued growth.

How and when we learn about sex affects the role it eventually plays in our lives. In ideal circumstances, learning about sex is closely tied to learning about affection and love. But this does not mean that we learn about all three simultaneously. In the order of human experience, affection precedes the other two. We are literally nurtured by affection during our first years after birth. As our parents touch, hold, caress, kiss, and fondle us during our infant and toddler years, we are being given our first knowledge of caring. We receive it without giving anything back. As we begin caring for our parents in return, we respond to their affectionate gestures with kisses and hugs of our own. Physical contact becomes something with which we are familiar and comfortable. It also becomes recognized as an external sign of the existing love-need satisfaction through our parents. If there has been no demonstration of love through our early years, affection takes on a distorted meaning of its own.

If we are deprived of physical affection during childhood—if our parents stop holding and touching us soon after infancy—then our adolescent years can be particularly confusing. Suddenly we experience sexual urges and *want* to touch other people. But we can't discriminate between affection and sexual stimulation. Not knowing (or not remembering) what it is like to be touched in the absence of the sexual drive, we cannot tell where to draw the line.

Our understanding of love comes after our understanding of affection. As we interact with our parents and watch them interact with each other, and as we experience their patience and understanding, we begin to comprehend that love is something that has to be worked at. We start to experience the tremendous satisfaction brought on by love-need fulfillment. And when our parents hug each other in front of us, we learn that affection can be a sign of that love-need satisfaction.

Our understanding of sex usually comes last—*after* we have developed an understanding of both affection and love. Having already learned about affection, we will be less apt to confuse friendly touching with sexual stimulation. Having already learned about love and the satisfaction of the love-need, we will be less apt to equate sex with the fulfillment of that need. We will more easily be able to tell when sexual behavior is and is not appropriate. *And we will more easily be able to deal rationally with our own sexual urges.*

We can show persons affection without loving them. But we cannot love them without showing some form of affection, whether physical or nonphysical. For sex to be perceived as having any tie-in with love, it must be preceded and accompanied by affection. A man who is seldom if ever affectionate toward his wife but wants lots of sex will be perceived by her as using her. A woman who never touches her husband outside of bed will have a hard time wanting or enjoying sex. People who do not know how to show affection, or do so with feelings of awkwardness, may find the sex act somewhat mechanical. If affection is a regular part of their day-to-day relationship, they will enjoy sex to its fullest—provided that love is present, too.

In other words, affection can be meaningful in the absence of love. Love can be meaningful in the absence of sex. *But sex cannot be meaningful in the absence of both love and affection.*

If we would only stop and think about this, we could save ourselves a lot of trouble and trauma in our lives. For example, we know that affection is something that can be given and taken fairly naturally. It's easy to show affection to someone we like. But is it easy to have sex with someone we like—as opposed to someone we love and have made a commitment to? Or do we find ourselves holding back?

And why do people hold back? What is there about sexual intimacy between strangers or even casual friends or uncommitted lovers that is so concerning? There seems to be a natural predisposition in humans to preserve their integrity until there is sufficient knowledge of another. When we violate that integrity, we tend to lose our sense of worth or value as a person. Sexual intimacy is not tied just to our love-need, but to all of our needs, and *especially our need for worth or dignity as a human being.*

The strong sexual urges we have as humans drive us to satisfying that urge through another, but what preserves us as humans is that in the process we fulfill our human needs of love, worth, belonging, enjoyment, and control as well. Our commitment to fulfilling our love-need through that person also preserves our worth-need fulfillment. Without that commitment, we allow ourselves to be used and to use others, and then drift on to someone else. Our worth-need fulfillment is preserved when those around us perceive us as having value as a person, and when we perceive ourselves and our actions as having value. What better way to destroy that sense of worth than to be perceived by others, as well as ourself, as someone to be used and then traded in, like a used car. *For a human body to be used in the name of "love" and then set aside for someone else's pleasure will tear at the very heart of our attempt to satisfy our need for worth.* When we want to experience sex and satisfy the urge, it should, for our own good, be accompanied by a committed attempt for love-need fulfillment. For sex alone will not only make it more difficult for future attempts at love-need fulfillment, it will affect our attempt at fulfilling our other human needs as well, especially our need for worth. In many persons I counsel, the tremendous lack of self-confidence and self-worth often can be traced to using others or being used sexually. So when *can* sex be enjoyed? When it doesn't in any way interfere with the fulfillment of any of our human needs as well as the needs of our partner.

Sex without affection and a committed love is nothing more than the stimulation of the sexual organs. This can create a very powerful and euphoric feeling, but it's not a feeling that lasts for long. By itself, sex is just another physical urge—like the desire to eat or drink. Like eating and drinking, it can be abused and cause us discomfort and misery.

Many years ago *Playboy* magazine surveyed its readers to find out who enjoyed sex the most. Not surprisingly, happily married couples came in first. And not,

I think, because they know more about sex than other people, *but because they were happily married, fulfilling all of their human needs through their marriage.* I would venture to guess that most of them viewed sex as a part of their lives together, and not as its focus. I would also venture to guess that their enjoyment of sex was due to a good amount of natural affection between them, along with a satisfying love- *and* worth-need fulfillment.

Even in a strong marriage, sex is likely to become routine and the pleasure the couple takes from it will diminish unless affection is always present to bridge the gap between sex and love. Affection is critical to maintaining a healthy relationship, and it should be continual and frequent. Hugging, kissing, touching, holding, and patting—all of these should be practiced on a daily basis. When affection is a habit, sex is more easily accepted and naturally enjoyed. Constant affection can be a positive and reassuring sign of love.

But affection is not a sign of love unless love is present. And sex in itself is never a sign of love. In fact, it has nothing to do with love. We may label the act of intercourse "making love," but it doesn't do a thing to build a love relationship. The intense feelings that accompany sex satisfy the sex-need, not the love-need, and the two are very different. Satisfying the love-need requires a conscious effort on the part of two people who have made a commitment to each other and to solving problems together. It involves a continual struggle, a willingness to work at getting along. Going to bed and having sex never solved anyone's problems. And it never satisfied anyone's love-need. Assuming that sex is enough to meet our love-need is like assuming that junk food is all we need to fulfill our nutritional needs. Either may create the illusion of satisfaction, but it won't fool our brain. Sooner or later, we'll feel dissatisfied with the way our life is going—a clear signal from our brain to change our ways.

We can enjoy affection for its own sake; the same cannot be said for sex. Affection is something we can show to almost anyone we meet—friends, parents, or even casual acquaintances. We can give a handshake, a pat on the back, a hug, or a kiss and come away with a warm feeling of friendship. Rarely if ever is a show of affection followed by a sense of disappointment.

Sexual intimacy, on the other hand, is by its very nature restrictive. If we deny its nature and pursue it for its own sake and especially if we try to use it to satisfy our need for love, we almost invariably feel let down afterward. We may experience intimacy during a sexual encounter, but once the pleasure subsides there is nothing left to sustain the intimacy. In fact, when the sex-need is satisfied, the desire for intimacy may be gone. When two people complete the highly stimulating sex act and there is no love between them to hold them together, they will separate. If sex is all they have in common, they won't have any reason to stay together. Genuine love lasts for twenty-four hours a day. How long can the enjoyment of a sexual encounter last?

One of the most dangerous illusions of sex is that it can be used to begin a love relationship. The truth of the matter is that premature sexual intimacy can lessen the chances that a love relationship will ever develop. Sex in the absence of love and affection creates any number of distorted perceptions. We come away thinking, "I feel so good; I must be in love," or "This person must care about me." Having sex too soon elevates sex to a position of importance it does not deserve. The couple, in turn, will perceive each other as sexual objects rather than as persons to be loved and cared for. Instead of working together to strengthen their relationship, they will pursue their individual pleasures at each other's expense. Love demands that we respect the other person's wants and needs; all sex demands is that we fulfill our own wants and needs. Love turns us outward toward others; sex without love turns us inward toward ourselves.

The inability to distinguish among love, affection,

and sex and assign each its proper role in a relationship is, I believe, one reason why so many people today are unable to achieve permanent love. But the *primary* reason why love is at such a premium is the distorted perceptions men and women have of each other.

More and more women are moving into the business world and gaining unprecedented economic and political power. These major sociological changes are being accompanied by major perceptual changes. Women are seeing themselves differently. They are valuing themselves at a higher level *in the work area* of their life. This is all to the good, but it would be even better if men's perceptions of women in this area had changed along with women's perceptions of themselves. Unfortunately, this doesn't seem to be the case.

In the social area, with the strong emphasis on sex— and on men and women as sexual objects—the media especially have contributed to the tendency on the part of both sexes to undervalue each other. The media have also given them a conflicting sense of their own value. In other words, men and women are being downgraded to little more than sexual objects in the social area of their lives while both, and especially women in the business and professional arena, are attempting to upgrade themselves in terms of their own worth. This conflict in worth between the work and social area can be devastating.

The problem is exacerbated by the fact that both men and women are now making themselves more easily accessible to each other as sexual partners. It is difficult for people to keep from developing an overinflated notion of their own importance when sex is so readily available. But those who view life as a sort of sexual smorgasbord never learn anything about love. And they never develop the positive perception of themselves— the *real* sense of their own value—that comes from loving and being loved.

Many men and women who hold to traditional sexual values are suffering severe internal conflict as well. Their perception of themselves (as having greater value) and society's perception of them (as sex objects) simply cannot be brought into harmony with each other. Furthermore, these persons are finding it very difficult to communicate to partners with differing values that they want to be seen for their true worth, and not merely as physically desirable. Too often, they face the monumental task of trying to find a secure, lasting, and loving relationship with someone having the same values—and decide it's not worth the effort.

There is no longer any need to make a commitment if what one wants is sex. Sex is everywhere. In its more subtle form, it stares out at us from billboards and magazine ads and waltzes across our TV screens a dozen times a day. In its most offensive form, it is found in the movie theaters and bookstores that deal in pornography. Perhaps the subtle form does greater harm because it is *more* accepted and *more* permeating. People seem to want the sexual illusions conjured up by the media without realizing that they create fantasy perceptions that lead nowhere.

Pornography gives us the worst possible impression of human relationships. And it is doing irreparable damage to our perceptions of ourselves as having value or worth. It solidifies our distorted perception of both men and women as sex objects and makes it that much more difficult for both to perceive each other and themselves as having value. Effectively and graphically, it teaches us how to use people without loving them.

If we begin a relationship by perceiving our partner as a sex object, and if we lack the ability to satisfy our love-need, where do we go from there? To another partner—and another. It is a sad comment on our throwaway culture that human beings are perceived as having so little intrinsic value.

Sex has a place in our relationships, but it's not the place we've currently assigned it. Sex should not be our first concern. When it is, we're going about things backwards. We're limiting our horizons at the outset. For it's very difficult to move from sex to love. On the other hand, it's relatively easy to move from love to sex. That should tell us something.

How can we go about returning sex to its proper place? By choosing to perceive people once again as having worth and value. By choosing persons through whom we can fulfill our love-need and by working hard at loving them and deserving their love.

Sex is a gift that can afford us tremendous pleasure throughout our lives. But if we only take that pleasure with no thought of giving it, it is short-lived and meaningless. To continually enjoy sex, and enjoy it to its fullest, we must place it within its rightful context by preceding it with love and affection. Having love and affection for another makes us want to please them. And working at pleasing another is the essence of love.

For a couple to derive the maximum enjoyment from sex, they must first work to develop a strong loving relationship and mirror that relationship in their affectionate behaviors toward each other. Once they have built their sexual intimacy on a firm foundation of love and affection, there will be no room for illusions.

6

The question of control

Perhaps the most difficult task we face in life is that of controlling for what we want while respecting the rights of others to do the same. To paraphrase an old saying, our freedom to satisfy our control-need ends where another person's nose begins. It's called responsibility. All we can really control are our own perceptions of the persons around us; we can change those perceptions to conform to what we want. We cannot, however, change others to conform to our perceptions—yet most of us seem to spend a lot of time and energy attempting to do just that.

People tend to control others when they are unable to responsibly self-control for their own human needs. In fact, *the need for control seems to be the need that is most abused and overused when humans aren't able to satisfy their human needs in any given area of their life.* If a spouse can't fulfill his or her human needs satisfactorily with the marriage, there is a tendency to try and get the other partner to conform to the way he or she wants them.

When we attempt to control others to get them to do what we want, whether we are successful or not, we are frustrated. Why? Because only *we* can satisfy our human needs by controlling our own world—*our* perceptions, *our* wants, and *our* behaviors. Our perception of our spouse is ours. It is in our head. We created it. And only we can change it. No one else can. Only we can control our perceptions.

A marriage *doesn't* need the attempt of one partner to control the other. Yet when one partner's needs aren't being met he or she will attempt to force the other into meeting them. Trying to control our partner isn't the answer. In fact, it is not only frustrating—it can't be done—it can also be devastating to the marriage because we are attempting to deprive our spouse of his or her need to self control. All we can control is what *we* perceive, want, and do.

I know that I very seldom try to control Hester, and I know why. My perception of her more than satisfies what I want, and what I do with what I want and now have, namely Hester, more than satisfies what I need. So there's no reason for me to attempt to dominate or change her. Why rock the boat? Her contribution is her willingness to continually work on her relationship with me—and the fact that she allows me to work at loving her. In that I am fortunate indeed. Living with someone who won't let you love him or her is like having food in the house and being unable to eat it. You wander around the house all day fighting off the pangs of hunger. With an uncooperative partner, the constant pain of loneliness can be unbearable, especially when the answer sits across the table from you. Unfortunately, love can't be forced on another. By its very nature, love demands freedom of choice.

I once counseled a woman who was desperate to keep her marriage together, even though it was patently obvious that her husband no longer loved her. Time and again, she literally threw herself at his feet. It took nearly two years before she was willing to relinquish her fantasy perception of him as the person she believed she could be happy with. How does it help to want someone who doesn't want you? What good does it do to subject yourself to constant rejection and pain? It is hard to take someone out of your world of wants when there is no one else.

When a couple does agree to work at staying together, the best thing they can do for their marriage is to strive not to control each other. On the surface, this may sound simple, but it can be one of the most difficult concepts to learn and live by. Although I espouse it to all of my clients, I have to confess that I don't always live by it myself. On occasions when things don't go exactly as

I'd like between Hester and me, I backslide and lash out at her with rude or cutting remarks—attempts at changing her when I should be focusing on changing my own perception of her and whatever she is doing that annoys me.

We all have certain ideas of how we want our spouses to be. We create perceptions based on those ideas. And then we *act* on those perceptions as though they were real.

In a marriage in which both partners perceive each other as satisfying their love-need, they usually find it unnecessary to try to control each other. Why change things when they're going well? But in a marriage where one partner perceives the other as *not* satisfying his or her love-need, this disparity between what he or she perceives (a critical or nagging partner) and what he or she wants (a loving, caring spouse) results in pain or stress. This in turn leads one partner to choose various behaviors to control the other person.

Police friends of mine who work the suburbs tell me that the single most frequent reason they're called is to intervene in family fights. What is the real reason why people yell and scream at one another or even physically abuse one another? The desire to control. If we perceive that someone doesn't love us or doesn't pay enough attention to us, what do we usually do? Anything we can think of to draw attention to ourselves and get our way. There's nothing that accomplishes this quite so effectively as picking a fight. Often it takes only a sly throwaway comment, like "We never go out anymore," or "You never pay attention to me," or "The only time you're nice to me is when you want sex." A few well-placed words, and we're off and running. We get the attention we're looking for—but is it the sort of attention that will satisfy our love-need? Hardly.

In a way, however, it does partially satisfy another need: our control-need. Starting a full-fledged argument or fight gives us the sense that we're in charge, that we're managing the show. Even though the "show" is a disaster, at least it temporarily masks the loneliness or powerlessness we may be feeling. For a while, it relieves some of the pain we're experiencing due to our unfulfilled love-need. It may also give us a slight sense of worth or belonging, since creating a disturbance around the house almost forces others to focus on us and respond to our demands. Sadly, some people lock themselves into believing that the limited satisfaction of their needs that they achieve by fighting is all they can expect from life. More than one person has told me, "Yelling at my wife (or husband) is the only thing that seems to work. If I don't yell, what else can I do?"

Another approach we take to controlling others is anger. Anger in itself—even without open fighting or arguing—can be devastatingly effective. If we slam doors, stomp around the house without speaking, meet inquiries about our mood with a stony silence or glare, or lock ourselves in a room, people will suddenly feel anxious about us. They'll leave us alone until our anger fades or do things for us in the hope of "making" us happy again, or tiptoe around us for fear of drawing our wrath upon themselves. In other words, they'll perform any number of behavioral calisthenics while we just sit there radiating bad feelings. Again, we are partially satisfying our control-need and worth-need, but at what price?

A more subtle way to control people is through depression. I believe that depression is a behavior we choose in an attempt to fulfill our unmet needs. Labeling it a sickness allows us to absolve ourselves of the responsibility of having chosen it. We look to others to "cure" us and make us better again rather than do it for ourselves.

To illustrate this idea, let's say that I drive my car to a grocery store, park, do some shopping, and come back to discover that someone has smashed in the front fender. I might (in fact, probably would) get depressed about this, but eventually I'd have to say to myself, "All right, what can I do to get the fender fixed?" I'd start by calling my insurance agent to find out whether or not my policy covered that type of damage. Then I'd call a repair shop and set up an appointment to have the fender fixed. Through these active, positive behaviors, I would eventually solve my problem, feel better as a result, and would no longer be depressed.

But what if I continued my negative perception of the incident? What if I let *myself* sink into a depression that lasted for days or even weeks—and, in the meantime, did nothing about having the car repaired? Eventually, Hester would feel sorry enough for me (or disgusted enough by my constant moping around) that she'd take care of the car for me. I would, in effect, have pushed the responsibility off on her. My depression would have had the result of her choosing to change her behavior— and that's the meaning of control.

Getting depressed is a programmed behavior. Like getting angry, it's something we learn early in life as a way of at least temporarily handling difficulties that arise. Often it's easier to shout or sulk than it is to set about figuring out what we need to do to solve whatever is bothering us. In one respect, depression isn't all bad. It sometimes affords us a little "breathing space," a period of time during which we can gather our strength to face our problems—much as grieving helps us to learn how to survive the loss of a loved one. But when we lock anger and depression into our behavioral system and they become our programmed responses to almost every conflicting situation, we're in trouble.

As noted earlier, we program many of our behaviors into our computerlike brains. If we didn't, we wouldn't be able to function. I know that I couldn't play tennis, or type, or drive if I had to think about every single move I made. Over the years, *we program many of our social behaviors as well.* Unlike those behaviors we use to improve our tennis game, though, these can't be easily evaluated as to which is best. I know that holding the racquet too loosely hurts my stroke; I'm not always sure when a social behavior is having the opposite effect of the one I'm intending. Few of us have the objectivity needed to perceive certain of our social behaviors as ineffective or even destructive. Usually, when things don't turn out as we want them to, we blame others.

We program many of the behaviors we use to relate to the persons around us just like the ones that enable us to get dressed in the morning and feed ourselves. For years, whenever I walked into the house and found my children fighting, I yelled at them to stop. If they didn't, I yelled all the louder. Did that help matters any? Of course not—but I seldom stopped to think about that. Yelling was what I had programmed myself to do, so I kept on doing it.

Why do we humans persist in behaviors like these that do us no good? I think we learn them. I'm not saying that my own parents yelled at me on a regular basis; I know that they didn't. But somewhere along the line, I got the idea that shouting was a good way to get someone to do what I wanted. Perhaps I tried it once, and it elicited the response I was looking for; often, it only takes one reasonably successful experience to firmly cement a particular behavior into our behavioral system. It's also likely that I may have learned how to yell by watching movies and television programs. Many of our behaviors are learned through what we perceive in the media.

What do we do with what we learn? In time, we teach it to someone else. For example, parents who grew up as abused children are very likely to abuse their own children when they come along. Parents who beat their children for misbehaving are teaching their children to beat others when they don't get what they want. But if abusive behavior is learned, so also is loving behavior. Children find out what love is primarily from their parents. When they receive warm and loving attention from their mother and father, and when they see their parents loving each other, they grow up believing that this is how people are supposed to behave toward one another.

When Hester and I touch, kiss, or embrace, we not only enhance our own relationship but also show our children how to express affection. When we take our evening walks together, go running in the morning, or leave town on occasion to share a weekend alone with each other, we are teaching our children what people in love do to stay in love. When we spend time with our children in shared, relationship-strengthening activities, we are imparting to them the basics of how our love-needs are satisfied.

I do things with my children—such as playing tennis with John, washing a car with Luke, or cleaning the garage with Thomas—for two reasons: first, because they fulfill my own needs for love and belonging, and second, because I know how valuable activities like these can be, and I want my sons to learn, too.

For some perverse reason, it's far easier to lock in a harmful, destructive, and controlling behavior than it is to change it. I struggled for years to find some other way of dealing with my children than yelling at them. Today, my family and I can look back at this and laugh. My children—especially Nelson and Luke—enjoy nothing more than mimicking "the way Dad used to be," and their favorite place for doing this is usually in the midst of a family gathering. Even I have to admit that their "mad Dad act" is pretty funny. At the same time, it reinforces my desire to be ever mindful of the way I behave around and toward my children. They remember so much of what we do!

As a counselor, I am constantly meeting couples who are miserable together precisely because they have locked themselves into controlling behaviors. They complain bitterly about how unhappy they are—yet they continue to do those things, day in and day out, that virtually guarantee that they'll stay unhappy. Most of the time, they're not even aware of the effects of their behaviors. They have no idea of how they perpetuate whatever problems they're having. Part of my role is to help them take a look at and evaluate what they're doing.

One young woman I counseled gave me this description of the man she was living with: Every night, he would come home from work, grab a beer, and sit in front of the TV until bedtime. I asked her whether she thought he was happy.

"Not at all," she said. "But that's what he does."

"Do you ever try to find out if there's something else he'd rather do?"

"Sure."

"And what does he say?"

"He accuses me of nagging him, gripes about his back, and tells me how his boss has been hassling him at work. Then he says there's nothing else he can do."

That clarified the reason behind his unhappiness, at least for me. He was spending all his time focusing on his perceptions of his wife, his back pains, and his boss, and none of it focusing on the real cause of his misery: his own behavior. He had resigned himself to having "no" control over his actions.

Recently I worked with a man who admitted to criticizing his wife far too much. "I know I do it, and after I do it I feel terrible," he told me. "But I keep doing it anyway. It just comes out of me before I can stop it." He didn't like his perception of his wife, and he didn't like his perception of himself. He had no idea that he could change both of those perceptions simply by looking at what he wanted, what he was doing, and by making a judgment and then a plan for improvement.

Another behavior we develop out of a desire to control others is sickness. I believe that most sickness is like depression: We can control it if we take responsibility for it. I'm not saying that all illness is self-induced—there are plenty of diseases that actually infect us—but I do maintain that much of the sickness we suffer, especially headaches, backaches, colds, and the like, are due to our inability to handle unresolved conflicts in our lives. And getting sick almost always has the result of making people pay attention to us. We learned this as children, when an ache or pain brought Mom or Dad running. If feigning sickness (or working ourselves into actually feeling sick) had the effect of releasing us from going to school or doing our chores around the house, we carry this behavior into our adult lives. Why not, since we had such success with it when we were young? Now any stressful occurrence brings on a nagging backache. Or we hear ourselves saying, "I don't feel well, honey. Would you mind taking care of the children for a while?" Or, "Not tonight—I have a headache."

When something we want conflicts with something we perceive, we can literally make ourselves sick over it. I know this from personal experience. I do some type of public speaking two or three times a week to classes I'm teaching, workshops I'm leading, or other groups who have invited me. I never use notes, preferring instead to leave room in my mind for new thoughts and ideas to come and go freely. Not long ago, I worked with the director of training of a local corporation on a course of instruction for the company's employees. While preparing the course, I took copious notes. When I was asked to give a lecture on the course to the company's officers, I decided for some reason to structure my speech around my notes. As I stood with my notes spread out in front of me on the day of my presentation, I suddenly found myself unable to hit my normal stride. By forcing myself to stick to my notes, I was preventing my mind from rearranging the ideas I wanted to discuss. Within about ten minutes, I had a splitting headache.

The following day, when I was scheduled to give the same lecture to another group, I did it in the way I was accustomed to and most comfortable with—without notes. And I sailed through it without even the suggestion of a headache. Looking back at what had happened the day before, I realized that my perception of what I was doing (giving a poor and rather jumpy talk) and what I wanted to be doing (giving a smoothly flowing talk) had been in conflict with each other, and this perceptual difference was handled by the physiological reaction within my body through a headache. If I had only tossed my notes aside, I might have solved my problem then and there. Instead, I had forced myself to continue what I was doing and, by extension, to maintain my high stress level. The second time I gave the lecture, my perception of what I was doing was consistent with what I wanted, and there was no reason for me to get a headache.

Although this example doesn't deal specifically with the issue of controlling others directly, it does illustrate that when we don't get what we want, and don't do anything about it, our brain will act to resolve the conflict in another way.

There are several behaviors besides fighting, anger, depression, and sickness that we use in our ongoing quest to control others. One of the most prevalent is guilt. Often, the less secure person in a relationship will use guilt as a tool for gaining power that is either slipping away or has never existed. An aging parent may complain to her grown and married daughter, "I never see you anymore. Don't you ever think about me? I'm so lonely!" Or a husband whose wife is on the verge of leaving him may say, "I've given you twenty years of my life, and now you're walking out. Think of the children!" Statements like, "I've been working hard all day— can't you take care of the car?" or "I'm overloaded. Can't you see that?" are all attempts to make others pay more attention to us, feel sorry for us, and do what we want them to do.

A single mother I have been working with on and off for several years is surrounded by persons who are constantly laying guilt on her. Her mother calls almost daily to say, "Dear, I've been up all night with your father. Could you stop by on your way home and fix us a meal?" or "You know, dear, I've almost forgotten what my grandchildren look like," or "It's such a nice day, and I'd love to get out of the house—why don't you take me shopping?" or "I'm not as good a driver as I used to be, and your father needs to get to the doctor. I made an evening appointment for him so you wouldn't have to take time off work." The woman's ex-husband, a practicing alcoholic who was injured some time ago in an industrial accident and claims that he still can't work, will call to level his own subtle guilt-inducing attacks. "Look," he'll tell her, "I'm not feeling well, and I haven't seen the children too much lately. Could you drop them off?" And then he'll add, "By the way, I'm out of food. Can you bring something for the kids to eat?"

Fortunately, my client is learning how to deal with both her mother and her ex-husband. She simply refuses to be controlled by the guilt they try to place on her. After listening patiently to her mother's demands for attention, she'll reply, "I know you want to get out, but I've made plans for today. Why don't you see if one of your friends will take you shopping?" And she'll counter her ex-husband's bids for control by responding, "Maybe you should wait to see the children until you're feeling better."

Often, we withdraw our love in the hope that this will get others to bend to our will. Recently I was at a shopping center when I observed a mother doing this with her young child: The child was crying her eyes out, hanging onto her mother's skirt, while her mother was saying to a friend, "I told her I was going to leave her for good if she didn't behave." This scene horrified me. Sure, the child was learning that she had to behave in public, but at what cost? We forget that children take us literally. Threatening a child with the loss of a parent is one of the worst things we can do to him or her. And what else was the little girl learning from her mother? That withdrawing love is a way to gain control over others.

One more way of attempting to control others is the stimulus-response approach—the stimulus being a gift, and the (desired) response being obedience or returned love. Adults often use this on each other, but the most common perpetrators are parents. The main problem with this approach is that it works only if the stimulus is perceived by the other person as worth responding to, and if the person on the receiving end is willing to do the specific desired behavior, as compared to other alternative behaviors. Another problem is that the response lasts only as long as the person is interested in what's being offered.

One of my clients—a woman with two children in their early twenties—has been going through a very sticky divorce. Her husband has moved in with a much younger woman and has started showering his son and daughter with gifts. One week it's a new car, another, a ski trip or a stereo. He knows that his children are upset and angry with the way he's treated their mother, and he's trying to buy back their affection. They aren't yet self-supporting, and they're undergoing substantial internal conflicts. On the one hand, they're tempted by their father's offerings and afraid of losing his "affection"; on the other, they struggle with their responsibility toward their mother. And what is the father doing? Teaching his children to control others with money and gifts.

I've described only a few of the techniques we use to get our way with other people; there are countless more. In one of the classes I teach, my students were able to come up with over fifty ways of controlling others that they had either experienced or considered using themselves. We withhold sex; we pout; we concoct elaborate verbal arguments that leave our listeners reeling; we mope around the house and refuse to talk about what's bothering us—the list goes on and on.

And what do we gain in the end from all of our attempts to control the persons we most want to love? Absolutely nothing. In fact, we stand to lose more from these behaviors than we had to begin with. Let's say we do manage to wear our partner down until he or she finally gives in to our every wish. What kind of relationship are we left with then? It is one in which the other person learns controlling by an expert; one which only seems to partially satisfy our control-need, is in constant danger of falling apart, and will never satisfy our need for love.

We all have the need to control. But the only way to really satisfy that need is by *controlling our own behavior, perceptions, and wants*. The sooner we realize this, the sooner we can begin to meet our control-need, *and* our love-need, *and* our belonging-need, and every other need that drives us.

The closer and more loving a relationship is, the less need there is for one or both partners to try to control the other. As I reflect on my own marriage to Hester, it seems to me that I make very few attempts to control her or she to control me. The more quality time we spend alone together, the less need there is to control.

One of the common myths about love today is that living together without being married allows each partner to exercise more control over his or her life. I would argue the opposite. Living together does give each person the option of walking out with fewer consequences than leaving a marriage, but does that do anything to help the relationship? And what about the sense of security that a firm mutual commitment brings? Knowing that Hester has decided to work at loving me, no matter what it takes, makes it much easier for me to fulfill my love-need through her.

In a close, loving, *committed* relationship, *no control exists*. Both partners are free to satisfy their own need. Both are free to pursue those things that interest and sustain them. Both are able to negotiate and compromise when circumstances warrant it. Neither has the desire to "correct" or "change" the other's behavior. Secure in themselves, in each other, and in their marriage, they can look forward to exploring the farthest reaches of love.

7

Criticism: the destroyer of love

Nothing kills the desire to love another more quickly or thoroughly than criticism. It is like a knife in our hands that we use to deeply wound the persons we most want to love.

There are two types of criticism: the blatant and the subtle. The first is like a sharp stab made in a moment of anger—"You're stupid," "You're incompetent," "You never do anything right." The second is like a nick from a razor blade—"Thanks for doing the dishes. Don't worry; I'll clean the sink," "You've put on a little weight recently," "Oh, so you didn't get that promotion after all?" The first type can really hurt. The second type, when experienced again and again, can tear another into pieces and shred whatever love he or she may have for us until there's nothing left. It can also make it difficult for those under attack to maintain feelings of self-worth and self-confidence.

Criticizing is a behavior that we all seem to learn sooner or later. People are always leveling little jabs and cracks at each other, and they seem so harmless and innocent on the surface. "I don't think you acted very nicely just then, dear," "You can be so annoying when you get upset," "You weren't very polite to my friends the other day," "I wish you could try to be more pleasant!" "I'm not criticizing you, honey; I'm only trying to help you understand what you're doing wrong," "Why do you keep acting that way?" We criticize our children, our spouses, our friends, our coworkers, our parents; no one escapes our pointed observations. And we suffer the same from them.

Why is criticism so terrible? The most obvious reason is because it hurts other persons. Even worse, in those

-105-

persons who perceive the criticism as a true reflection of their own inadequacy, it will create a tremendous internal conflict. This is especially true if those same persons are working hard to change their perceptions of themselves and fulfill responsibly their own human needs. In order to be caring and loving toward others, I must perceive myself as a caring and loving person. If I see myself as inadequate in these areas—as most of us do—then cutting remarks from others only serve to confirm my perception of inadequacy and make it that much more difficult for me to change my perception of myself.

Recently my daughter Terry asked me if I would take her to the hardware store so she could buy some electrical supplies for her house. I was busy at the time, and I told her no. Later, as I thought about it, I didn't like what my rejecting behavior did to my perception of myself as a father. I usually consider myself a pretty good father. I suddenly found myself wondering if refusing my daughter's request was the best thing to do.

I went to Hester and told her that I'd changed my mind; I had decided to drive Terry to the store after all. In response, Hester said, "Thank you dear. I'm sure she will be pleased." But what if she had said, "Well, why didn't you say yes in the first place?" or "Please don't be grumpy with her just because she interrupted your afternoon. You know how you sometimes are." Either of those remarks would have made it harder for me to return to my positive perception of myself as a father. I might have spent the rest of the afternoon mulling over the reasons why Hester had so little faith in me. *This would have reinforced the unloving, uncaring perception of myself that I wanted to correct.*

Criticism never accomplishes what we want it to. We deceive ourselves into thinking that it's all right to tell another person when he or she is doing something wrong or not meeting our expectations. We may not intend any harm by our "I'm-perfect-and-I'm-trying-to-straighten-you-out" remarks, but harm is the end result.

I behave according to how I perceive myself and others. *I also behave according to how I believe others perceive me.* How Hester perceives me is especially important, since she's the person through whom I most want to satisfy my love-need. If she were constantly telling me that I was wrong about this or that, that I was a disappointment to her, or that I needed to change, I would not only have to overcome my negative perception of myself but take on the added burden of overcoming her negative perception of me. Meanwhile, I would find it almost impossible to be loving and caring toward her, because my perception of her (as someone who didn't believe in me) would conflict with how I wanted to perceive her (as someone who had faith in me), and this perceptual difference would create within me more pain or stress.

What's the best way to handle criticism from our loved ones? By ignoring it—if we can. But this presupposes an inner strength on our part and a healthy self-confidence in our behavioral system. One thing is certain: We should never respond to criticism in kind, since this can only make matters worse. When we start hurling barbs back, this confirms and adds fuel to our critics' negative perception of us. And considering that they must have a negative perception to begin with, or they probably wouldn't have criticized us, this makes it even harder for them to return to the point at which they can begin thinking positively about us once more. They might also perceive us as trying to control them, which will further solidify their negative perceptions of us.

In short, it's best to tread softly. Give them time to cool down and relax; avoid confronting them at all costs. If you must say something then and there, try asking for help. For example: "Honey, I don't know what to say. I want to be happy with you. What do you want for us? Let's talk about what we can do to work things out between us." When you respond in this way, you make it easier for them to reconcile what they have just done with what they know they should do. When they perceive you as supporting and noncritical, they can begin to move toward you in a caring and loving way without fear of retribution.

We all have the human need to control our own lives. Too often, this splashes over into efforts to control other persons' lives as well. Criticism is only one of the many techniques we use to accomplish this. Statements like, "I don't think you can handle that," or "What did you do that for?" or "You should know better," or "How many times do I have to tell you?" are really nothing more than veiled attempts to get people to change. In effect, we're telling them that they're not all they should be. What does that do to their perceptions of themselves? If they are confident enough to begin with, they will maintain a positive perception of self and choose behaviors to handle the problem effectively. If criticism is characteristic of the relationship, eventually the person will form negative perceptions of either self or other or both, ultimately giving up on self or the relationship.

How do we get into the behavior of criticizing others? We learn it from those around us. Like brushing our teeth, or driving a car, or eating, or putting our socks on, criticizing is a behavior we have learned and programmed. Instead of changing our perception to conform to what we want to perceive, we mistakenly believe it's "him" or "her" we must change, for then we'll be happy. Unfortunately, attempting to change those around us leads us on a short route to frustration. We watch others doing it with some measure of success, and we start doing it too. And if we manage to get something we want by being critical, we lock into this behavior, but ultimately we are disillusioned.

I know a teenaged girl who has developed a whole series of behaviors to draw upon whenever she wants something. For example, if she wants to borrow her father's car, she gives him a hug and says softly, "Hi, Dad. How's things?" If she wants to get out of cleaning her room—something her mother usually tells her to do—she yells, screams, and finally stomps out of the house and slams the door. She uses these behaviors because they work for her, and she'll keep using them until they no longer do—in other words, until her parents stop allowing themselves to be controlled by her.

There's a big difference between this type of outright controlling behavior and criticism, however. The object of controlling behavior is to coerce someone into *doing something for us*; the object of critical behavior is to coerce others into *changing their behavior by "making" them feel bad about themself.*

Let's say that Hester leaves the house to run errands and neglects to say hello to me when she returns. I might perceive her actions as a sign that she's not paying enough attention to me and then choose to be upset. I might say, "Well, hello to *you*, too!" Knowing Hester, she'd probably reply, "Oh, I'm sorry, honey. I wasn't thinking," and walk over to give me a kiss. Other people might snap back with equal vigor, though, and we'd be off and running in a mutual sniping session.

Criticism is a tactic we employ to get people to change what they are doing or even something about themselves—the way they treat us, an opinion they hold dear, the way they look or act or think. Underlying this attempt to control is the assumption that we know better than they do what's good for them. And this is an assumption we have no right to make. Through criticism, we deny others the freedom to take responsibility for their own lives. By making judgments about everything they do rather than accepting them as they are, we are insinuating that they are incapable of taking care of themselves or making reasoned decisions, or belonging with us. Even when we perceive a partner acting irresponsibly, criticism never helps solve the problem, because *it doesn't teach a better way in an accepting atmosphere.*

I personally find it very frustrating when someone corrects me or tells me when I'm doing something wrong. I usually know when I've goofed, and I prefer being left alone to figure out how to amend the situation; I don't need other people to do that for me, and I find it hard for me to internally resolve my own conflict when they try. When I snap at Hester, I know I've made a mistake. When I ignore my children's requests to play with them, something inside me urges me to reconsider. When I behave badly toward someone, my internal monitoring system kicks in and I feel guilty or remorseful. The last thing I need is for someone else to add to my guilt or remorse. My chances of being able to correct my own behavior—and, hence, change my perception of my-self—are reduced if another person comes along with a cutting remark.

We may think we're doing people a favor when we draw their attention to their errors. We fail to realize that although people are often unaware at the time that what they're doing is ineffective, they must be allowed the time to reconcile what they are doing within themselves. Their behavior is so obvious to us that we presume it's also obvious to them, which is seldom the case. Rarely can I predict the full consequences of something I choose to do; it's only *after* I've done it that these consequences become clear to me. The feelings that result from my need-satisfaction tell me whether it was a helpful thing to do or not. But these feelings *follow* the action, they don't *precede* it. If they are then colored by criticism from someone else, it distracts my thinking and makes it that much harder for me to evaluate what I have done and learn a better way. I may then become more intent on defending and maintaining my perception of myself instead of correcting my behavior. Criticism by another focuses our attention on our perception of self, rather than on our behavior.

Most of us just bumble through life, trying to do the best we can. Few of us set out to purposely hurt other people. When we do hurt them, we are just trying to change our perception and we do so, often quite naturally, without evaluating our behavior. We all slip up; it's human nature. Criticism carries with it the implication that we're always conscious of our behaviors when, in truth, so much of what we do we have programmed and we think little of its impact on others.

A few seconds of criticism can destroy hours or even days of positive perceptions. I give many workshops, and people who attend them seem to appreciate and enjoy what I have to say. I work hard to maintain a caring, supportive atmosphere in each group I work with. But what if, during the question-and-answer session at the end of an otherwise successful workshop, I were to turn to someone and say, "That was a stupid question" or "I think the answer to that is rather obvious"? I would instantly turn what had been a pleasant experience into a bad memory for everyone there. Similarly, if a couple spends a close and loving weekend together away from home, and on the way back one partner tosses off a nasty comment, this can be enough to undo the good they accomplished during their time alone together.

When we really love others, we accept them as they are. We make our love visible through little acts of kindness, shared activities, words of praise and thanks, and our willingness to get along with them. Attempts to change them, correct them, and shape them into how we want them to be aren't acts of love. They're acts that shake love's very foundations. Criticism, regardless of its intent, can only undermine the love that two persons have for each other.

I know some couples who are literally afraid to talk with each other about many things. Why? Because in the past, attempts at conversation have resulted in criticism in certain areas of their life. They begin to avoid these areas. They also avoid doing things with each other for fear that their every action will be criticized as well. Eventually, they quit talking and doing things together. This is not the way a marriage—or any other kind of relationship, for that matter—should operate.

When Hester and Dorothy opened their poster gallery, they were full of excitement and eager to draw me into what they were doing. One day, they invited me to help them mount posters in the back room. The first thing I said when I walked in was, "This place is a mess!" In my perception, it *was* a mess; it seemed cluttered and disorganized. But what right did I have to criticize them? Did that help them to run their gallery more efficiently? Or, even more important, did it help our relationship any? As soon as I shut my mouth, these questions flooded into my mind, and immediately I became conscious of what I had said.

My son Joseph also noticed the way the gallery looked. But, I'm embarrassed to admit, he handled the situation far better than I. He quietly told Hester and Dorothy some ideas he had about reorganizing things and, with their permission, set about implementing them. He mananged to put the gallery in order without ruffling anyone's feathers. In fact, this experience enhanced his relationships with his mother and sister.

When I'm critical of my family, it is very hard for me to act loving and affectionate toward them. Sometimes, if I don't like something that Hester or one of our children is doing, I have to force myself to perceive that behavior indifferently. I have to force myself to perceive the person nonjudgmentally. This change of perception is followed by a behavior change, as the anger and the criticism recede. With an indifferent perception, I can then approach the issue calmly and rationally.

Our family is very close primarily because we're all willing to work at getting along with one another. This isn't easy, and it takes a great deal of effort on everyone's part, but it's worth it. What happens, though, when people aren't willing to work at getting along? What if, for example, your spouse simply refuses to do things with you, talk with you, or take an active part in holding your relationship together?

If you have serious problems with your spouse, and it doesn't look as if things are going to change, then it will be up to you to make some choices. At all costs, avoid criticizing him or her, or you'll ruin any chance you may have had for a reconciliation. Instead, consider your options. You may want to seek help from an impartial third party, such as a counselor. You may try negotiating with your partner, keeping in mind that this can be time-consuming and disappointing. You may attempt to manipulate your partner into changing, but your controlling behavior will more likely than not create a whole new set of problems. Or you may decide that living apart is preferable to living together. Often, a separation can be beneficial. It gives both persons time to reflect without being pushed, allows them the freedom to work things out on their own and the time to build sufficient strength needed when they move back together again. When separated couples are ready to resume living together, they should first spend quality time alone together on a regular basis while still apart. Once their love-needs are perceived by both as being satisfied sufficiently so that difficulties can more easily be resolved, then renewed intimacy can be more easily tolerated.

We don't always know when we make mistakes, but most of the time we do; our sensing of a lack of need-fulfillment tells us. So do the consequences of ineffective behaviors. What enables us to correct our mistakes is the presence of another person who believes in us and trusts that we are capable of resolving our own conflicts and successfully controlling our own lives. This can be the role of a spouse or a friend. And this is also the role of a counselor, one who cares, has faith in his or her clients, and teaches. If we are surrounded by persons who criticize and belittle us, we will never learn to believe in ourselves and perceive ourselves as having value.

I have absolute confidence and faith in Hester, and I tell her so often. My perception of her is important to her. By the same token, I give our children as much encouragement and support as I can. I am constantly letting them know through my words and actions that I am sure of their abilities to make something of themselves and do whatever they want to do with their lives. This sometimes means swallowing a critical remark or choosing not to perceive a behavior I don't approve of. But I can see in all of my children, every day, the positive effects of how I (and Hester) relate to them. Just as I did when I was growing up with two loving parents, my children are beginning to develop in areas they never even dreamed possible.

I have chosen Hester as the person through whom I want to fulfill my love-need. I perceive her as someone through whom I will always want to fulfill my love-need. The only thing that could change this would be a change in my perception of her. If she were to start criticizing me, it would become more difficult for me to maintain my positive perception of her. It would be more difficult for me to keep loving her. If I choose to perceive her as a critical person, it would conflict with the way I wanted to perceive her, namely as a loving and caring person, and it would be much harder for me to fulfill my love-need through her. Her criticism would make it hard for me to perceive myself as having value.

Criticism destroys love like cancer destroys healthy cells. Why, then, do we criticize? We do it because we have learned to do it as a way to control others, to turn them into the persons we want them to be, to make them make us happy. As if anyone else could change us or make us happy! Happiness comes from within; it is something we create in ourselves. No one else can do it for us.

Built into each of us is the need to control and the power to satisfy all our needs by taking charge of our own lives. Reaching beyond ourselves and attempting to control other people's lives is a misuse of that power. It frustrates their control-need and deprives them of the right to make their own choices and decisions.

Humans aren't made to be controlled; we aren't objects or machines to be used by others at their will. We are thinking, wanting, feeling, behaving, perceiving beings, and each of us is unique. But we all have something in common: We all need someone to love who accepts us as we are—complete with our inadequacies and hangups, opinions and prejudices, silly habits and eccentricities. Someone who isn't always trying to manipulate us and who can be patient with us as we struggle internally to grow and change. Someone who won't keep digging up past events—which can never be undone—and throwing them in our faces. Someone who overlooks our many mistakes and expresses in words and actions his or her continuing belief that we can and will make it. Someone who can forget. Someone who values us and, by so doing, makes it possible for us to value ourselves.

8

Creating love in your world

Sam and Peg had been married for nearly thirteen years when they came to see me. Sam was in his mid-forties and had his own home repair business; Peg was in her mid-thirties and worked in the mornings as a receptionist in a doctor's office. Both were recovering alcoholics, and both had been married before. They were raising four children together: two from Peg's prior marriage, and two of their own.

Recently a problem had arisen between them that needed solving, and they had decided to seek help since they hadn't been able to come to an agreement on their own. Basically, Peg wanted to visit her mother for a week, and Sam didn't want her to go. He admitted almost immediately to being a very controlling person who was incensed by her desire to leave him alone when he was clearly opposed to it.

"How could she even think of such a thing?" Sam asked, glaring at Peg. "Her place is in our home. She has no business running off to see her crazy mother."

Sam's anger, I soon learned, was typical of his behavior throughout their marriage. He used it to control Peg and the children; how angry he chose to get on a given occasion depended on how far they had gotten "out of line."

As is the case with any couple I agree to work with, I began by asking Sam and Peg if they really wanted to work at their marriage. They said that they did. We then moved to a general discussion of the specific things they did together that they perceived as helpful to their marriage. I found out that about the only activity they shared on a regular basis was sex. They would both come home from work each day at noon, eat, then go to bed. Then

Sam would head back to work at around two o'clock, and Peg would spend the rest of the day alone in the house.

That they had sex daily didn't give us much to work with. More important was the fact that they seemed honestly committed to staying together. This gave us a basis for developing a plan that included a number of shared activities aimed at rebuilding their fragile relationship. During the next three to four weeks, they increased the amount of time they spent alone together by taking evening walks, cooking their noon meal together, and playing card games after the children had gone to bed.

With most couples, activities of this type have the effect of establishing a closeness that reduces the number of angry outbursts and cuts down on upsetting behaviors. Spending quality time alone together begins to change their perceptions of each other from negative to positive. For Sam and Peg, however, it wasn't enough. Only a little improvement could be seen. Sam stayed angry, just not as often. And Peg still found it hard to be loving and caring toward him in the face of his somewhat reduced harping and criticism.

When I discussed this with Sam alone, he said, "I know, I know, it's my problem. Somehow I can't help getting angry with her. I just don't think it's right for her to leave me to see her mother." (He still hadn't gotten around to deciding whether or not Peg would follow through on her plans.) "To tell the truth," he went on, "I don't even like her working. When I start earning enough money on my own business, I'm going to make her quit her job."

I was puzzled. Normally, couples who make the effort to spend more time alone together begin to change noticeably after the first few weeks of shared activities. But Sam was still as abusive toward Peg, and Peg was retreating from him. Quality time alone together seems to turn couples around according to how strong they are. The weaker the marriage, the longer it takes.

I decided to look closely at the fact that they were both recovering alcoholics. When people drink excessively, they do it to reduce the pain or the perceptual difference between what they want (in Sam's case, a happy marriage) and what they perceive (an unhappy marriage). Alcohol—or any other drug—can only partially and temporarily reduce the pain. It cannot do the most necessary thing, that is, bring about a complete change in a person's perceptual and behavioral patterns. Recovering alcoholics I know tell me that quitting drinking is *only* the beginning. The single greatest challenge most recovering alcoholics face is the need to raise their level of self-confidence, which is usually perilously low. As practicing alcoholics, they have grown accustomed to a distorted perception of themselves and, if they have families, of their spouses and children. Because they have quit drinking doesn't mean they have changed their perception of themselves or their family; it only means they have quit drinking. I have been told it takes at least five years before they can expect to fulfill all their needs satisfactorily. In short, they have to learn to live all over again. The fact that they have stopped drinking isn't sufficient to rebuild a sense of worth. Their whole life has to be perceived as need-fulfilling and satisfying.

Persons who manage to change their drinking behaviors don't necessarily change other programmed behaviors or programmed perceptions at the same time. They play old tapes over and over again. Sam perceived himself as unloved. When Peg kept him at a distance, this only reinforced his perception of himself—as well as his perception of her as uncaring and unresponsive. His anger followed his perceptions as night follows day. Changing his angry behaviors without first changing his negative perceptions is very difficult indeed. The easier road is in changing perceptions through specific behaviors.

Not that Peg was totally innocent in the meantime; quite the contrary. She had her own programmed behaviors and perceptions. Whenever Sam got angry, this confirmed her perception of him as a so-and-so. Her programmed response was to get cold and more critical of him—and away they both would go into another round of behavioral antics.

In a way, the two of them were made for each other. Their unhappy, misery-producing behaviors meshed perfectly. For them, spending quality time together wasn't totally the answer; I knew that quality alone time was necessary. It just wasn't enough. They needed more help, added to quality alone time, before they could live happily together.

What I determined to do, along with continuing their quality time, was to get them to work on a plan to change their perceptions of each other and, by extension, of themselves—to see each other (and themselves) as the good, fine persons they are. By so doing, I hoped to enable them to pull themselves up out of the destructive cycle they had gotten into and move into a more positive cycle that would eventually prove self-perpetuating.

* * *

We satisfy most of our basic human needs through interacting with others. My love-need is fulfilled by loving and being loved. My belonging-need is met by successfully interacting with the people around me. My need for enjoyment is met when Hester and I, or my children and I, or my friends and I have fun together.

My need to value myself—my need to have a strong and healthy sense of self-worth—is satisfied when others notice and praise the things I do and when I am chosen to be a part of their lives. Knowing how fulfilling it is when someone takes an interest in me, I am careful to take an interest in the persons I love. I regularly ask one of my daughters, Mary Ellen, what she thinks about the psychology courses she is taking in college and commend her when she does well. I ask another daughter, Terry, how her young son (my grandson) Thomas is doing under her loving parenting. I will go to one son,

Joseph, for advice on a real estate transaction and another, John, for advice on a computer I'm considering purchasing. In all of these instances, I am aware that I help my children enhance their perceptions of themselves.

This is not to say that people should stand around endlessly heaping praise on one another; too much of this becomes phony. But behaviors like asking others for their help, expressing a sincere desire to find out what they think, and making it clear that we need and treasure their presence and assistance can go a long way toward helping ourselves fulfill our needs while allowing others to fulfill their needs through working at getting along with us. *Equally important, these behaviors enhance our perceptions of others and cause us to view them more positively.*

* * *

With Sam and Peg, as with most other couples I counsel, I began the process of trying to help them change their perceptions of each other by working with them individually. (I see some couples together.)

The first time I saw Sam alone, he admitted that he loved Peg very much. He also admitted to being too critical of her—while attempting to justify his critical attitude in terms of things she did.

"Do you think that criticizing her is helping matters any?" I asked.

"Let me tell you about something she did just the other day . . ." he began.

"I'm really not interested, Sam. All I want to know is whether you think criticizing her is helping you get along with her."

"Ed," he said, "I know I shouldn't be acting that way. But I keep doing it anyway. I just can't help it."

In a sense, he was right. As long as he maintained his negative perception of Peg, it was nearly impossible for him to change his behavior toward her. And as long as he kept feeding that perception by noticing only the "bad" things she was doing, there was no way he could begin to curtail his verbal attacks on her.

"Isn't there something I can do about this?" he asked. "Something I can do on my own, without having to deal directly with her?"

Given his willingness to work at their marriage, we were able to develop a plan. It consisted of his keeping a *daily written account* of the *good* things he saw Peg do. We set two rules: First, he had to list two things every day; and second, he couldn't repeat himself—meaning that he had to come up with two *new* things each time he sat down to write.

The primary purpose of this exercise was to level a direct assault on Sam's negative perception of Peg. He would start filtering out the "bad" behaviors he was used to seeing by forcing himself to notice "good" ones instead—two different good ones each day. The exercise would also serve a purpose within the context of our counseling sessions by giving both Sam and me a chance to look over and review the sorts of things he was perceiving.

The list he handed over to me during our next session contained observations like, "She said good night to me," "She cooked me a great meal," "She was nice to me," "She dresses well."

"Looks good," I told him, "but most of what you've written here is pretty general. You're going to have to get more specific.

"Try pretending you're a screenwriter," I suggested. "You're working with a director, and you're trying to tell him exactly how you want a certain actress to stand, and move, and deliver her lines—the lines you wrote. Visualize Peg doing a certain thing or being a certain way. Then list those instances when your visualization matches up to what she actually does."

His second week's list was far more elaborate and specific than the first. On it he had written, among other things, "She had dinner on the table at 6 P.M.," "She bought an attractive coat this afternoon," "She kept the kids away from the newspaper until I had a chance to read it."

While we were going over his list, Sam said something very interesting: "I don't know what it is, but I didn't get angry with her very much this week. And when things were going well, we seemed a lot closer than we've been for a long time."

He then pulled a small bound notebook out of his pocket and handed it to me. "I bought this to keep my daily lists in," he said, smiling. "I'm going to keep looking for things she does that I like, and I'm going to write them down in here. When it's full, I'm going to give it to her as a gift."

Clearly, we were on the right track!

About halfway through our session, I decided to shift the focus somewhat by asking if there was anything else he wanted to discuss.

"Well," he began, "I still don't feel very good about myself."

As we talked further, I learned that he had a problem common to most recovering alcoholics: a very low self-image. Here was a man who had been able to admit to being chemically dependent, look for help, commit to being helped (he had spent time in a treatment clinic), dry out, and stay sober for ten months. During that time, he had rebuilt his business, gone to weekly Alcoholics Anonymous meetings, and begun gluing his family life back together. Yet his low self-image persisted. He still saw himself in terms of all the wrong things he had done in the past.

"You'll need a second notebook," I told him.

"What for?" he wanted to know. "I haven't even started this one!"

"This week, I want you to begin keeping another list—one of good things *you* do. The same rules apply: Write down two specific things every day, make sure they're two new things, and don't repeat what you've written on any of the preceding days."

"Then what?" Sam asked.

"Who knows?" I answered. "Maybe when it's full you'll want to give it to yourself as a gift!"

* * *

In working with Sam and Peg, I discovered how useful and revealing list-keeping can be, and I have since employed this technique with many of my other clients. The results have invariably been positive, and the process has almost always been the same with each person. Everyone begins by listing very general perceptions— "He listens with an open mind," "She can laugh," "He loves his children"—and has to be prodded into making more pointed and relevant observations.

Recording on paper that someone is "nice" or "looks good" or is "considerate" doesn't mean much to the writer. Words like these could describe any number of people and *don't reflect the kind of effort needed to find and acknowledge good behaviors—without which a negative perception can't change.*

Compare "He was nice to me" with "He called me this morning to tell me he was thinking about me and couldn't wait to see me this evening." Or "She loves our children" versus "She spent an hour playing backgammon with our son." Specific observations of the second type make the person seem more real. A whole collection of them can serve as the basis for a genuine perceptual change.

The list-keeping exercise can be used under almost any circumstance. I recently counseled a woman who was separated from her husband. After ascertaining that the two of them viewed the separation as temporary and were willing to work at their marriage, I asked the woman to begin writing down her husband's good behaviors.

"How can I when he's not around?" she wanted to know.

"Do you talk on the telephone? Does he come by to see you?"

"We call each other almost every day. And he does stop by the house every other day."

"Then use the time you spend on the phone to find out what he's doing. And watch him more carefully when he visits."

When we write down our own specific behaviors, we become more conscious of actions.

I do business consulting as well as family and personal counseling, and I recommend a similar exercise to supervisors who want to learn to use their time more efficiently. When they record their daily activities at fifteen-minute intervals, they can quickly identify those periods when they aren't making the best use of their time and can make the appropriate adjustments to their schedules. Remember, we rarely think of and make judgments about what we do. When we write down what we do, it forces us not only to become more conscious of our behavior but also to evaluate it.

My favorite list-keeping stories, however, come from people who have used this technique to improve their marriages. One woman I worked with admitted that she almost never touched her husband. She had tried more than once to change her behavior but had always reverted to her old ways. She loved her husband, and she wanted to be more affectionate toward him; somehow, though, she just had difficulty behaving physically in a loving way.

I recommended that she consciously touch him twice each day and keep a written record of when, how, and where she touched him. She found that the list not only helped her to continue her efforts but also affected how she perceived herself. As reaching out to her husband became easier and more enjoyable, her pleasure during sexual intercourse increased. She started taking a more active and aggressive role during sex, and her whole outlook changed for the better.

Recently I have begun carrying this idea of list-keeping further with some of my clients. Along with asking them to record good behaviors they notice in their spouse and themselves, I have them do a full-scale inventory of their marriage.

We begin by focusing on *wants* ("Do you want to stay married? If so, do you want to let things go on as they are or make them better? If not, do you want to get a divorce? What are the consequences of your choices?"). We then move to perceptions ("What is your perception of an ideal marriage? How do you perceive your spouse? What are his or her positive qualities?"). Finally, we examine their behaviors ("What are you doing to help your marriage? What are the shared activities you do with your spouse? Which activities do you believe help the most? Name some activities you would be willing to do."). Again, I ask them to be specific, and to write their responses on paper.

In effect, this exercise lays their whole married world out in front of them. When it is there in writing for them to see, they can evaluate their own wants, perceptions, and behaviors efficiently. And they can develop more effective plans for the future.

In order to change ourselves from the way we *perceive* we are to the way we *want* to be, we must literally force ourselves to pay attention to everything we do. And because the majority of our behaviors are programmed, this can make certain tasks suddenly very difficult to perform. If you're a fast typist, and you decide one day to concentrate on where each of your fingers falls on the keyboard, your typing will slow to a crawl. The same holds true for playing the piano or, for that matter, playing a sport. We simply aren't meant to turn our conscious gaze on every little thing we do. If we did, we'd never accomplish anything. Watching a movie of what we do, hearing our voice on tape, writing down our thoughts or behaviors—all of these have a powerful effect on us because they force us to literally perceive what we are doing. It is like forcing ourselves to look at our behaviors in a mirror. We can no longer escape the reality of what we're doing. Once we evaluate how we perceive our various behaviors, it then allows for a reasonable plan to improve.

Interestingly, what we are most aware of in others, namely their behavior, we are least aware of in ourselves. Conversely, what we are most aware of in ourselves, our perceptions and our wants, we know practically nothing of concerning others.

Our programmed behaviors make it possible for us to operate efficiently in our complicated world. The problem arises when these behaviors don't work to our advantage. We then have to make the effort to reprogram our computerlike brains with new behaviors. And, as Sam and Peg both learned, this can be a long and involved process.

* * *

Sam agreed to buy another notebook and follow my suggestion that he write down two good things he did every day. After nearly three weeks, he was beginning to see a little progress. Also, he and I had formed a friendship, and he trusted me enough to keep trying.

During that period, I also started seeing Peg alone. The first time we talked, it became evident that she had decided for some reason to stop working at their marriage. It was almost as if she was standing on the sidelines of a game only Sam was playing. She wasn't sure what the outcome would be, and she wasn't doing anything to influence it.

"Peg," I asked her, point-blank, "do you really want this marriage to work?"

"I guess I really don't know the answer to that," she said. "Things aren't going as well as they could be—and yet Sam is trying awfully hard."

"What about you? Are you trying?"

"Not as much as I should," she admitted.

"Well, what do you want to do? Work at your marriage, stay miserable, or get a divorce?"

I went on before she could answer.

"You have a man, better than some, no worse than others, who's trying to work at loving you. You have thirteen years in your marriage, several children, and a husband who's trying to rebuild what little love there is between you into something more. And you've got someone—me—who's willing to teach you both.

"But I can't help you if you don't want this marriage to continue. I can't make you want what you don't already want. So," I ended, "what *do* you want?"

"When you put it that way," she said, "I suppose I'd be a fool not to work at it for a while. Even if we don't end up staying together, at least I can say I tried. And if we do, I'll have a happy marriage."

This conversation marked the beginning of some real improvement. Like Sam, Peg started keeping two notebooks—one for recording his good behaviors, and the other for recording her own.

Several weeks went by before the two of them met with me at the same time.

"I think we're getting somewhere," Sam reported. "We still argue, but our arguments last for minutes instead of days."

"And we get over them much more quickly, too," Peg added.

Both admitted that their marriage was better than it had ever been—even when compared to the first few months they had spent together.

"It sure is hard, though," Sam observed. "I never thought that loving someone took so much work!"

* * *

Another way to improve our perceptions of the persons we want to love is by doing things just to please them. Often, I fix dinner and have it on the table when Hester comes home from work. Or I buy her a flower, or make our bed in the morning, or open her car door for her. Frankly, I like perceiving myself as the sort of person who does pleasing things.

It's important to monitor our motives when we do things for others, however. It's very tempting to do them out of a hidden desire to manipulate or control them—to "make" them happy, or "make" them love us, or coerce them into conforming to our image of them. Doing something nice for another person while expecting a specific response from them is like giving a gift with strings attached. Doing it freely helps us to satisfy our own love-need. Looking for a response shifts the entire act to one of control of our spouse. If it happens to evoke a positive response, we should accept it for what it is, a pleasant response. The pay-off comes from our own effort at fulfilling our own need-satisfaction.

For example, if I put my arms around my daughter Dorothy and hug her whenever I see her, does this give me the right to expect her to hug me back every time? No, it doesn't. She might in fact do that—she usually does. Then again, she might pull away, or she might look at me, smile, and say, "Hi, Dad." If I catch her when she is preoccupied with something, she might return my gesture with a brief squeeze while saying, "Later, okay?" All I can control is what *I* do. When I hug her, it has to be because *I* want to do it, because it helps *me* satisfy my own love-need.

Ultimately, it is up to each of us to create love in our own world of wants, perceptions, and behaviors. When we make up our minds to do this by working to form positive perceptions of those we love, and by developing the habit of doing things to please them, something very interesting happens. We begin to gain more control over our lives and to feel much more satisfied with how our own needs are fulfilled. In other words, we not only fulfill our love-need but our control-need as well.

Needless to say, this requires time and effort—and often a great deal of both. With some couples I have counseled, it has taken many months before they have reached the point at which they were no longer in danger of reverting to their old, harmful perceptions and behaviors whenever the opportunity arose. And not all couples have chosen to stay together. Does this mean that they have "failed"? I don't think so. More than once, I have watched a couple separate and divorce with much more ease and with much less pain and stress than they might have experienced had they not first learned that they are in control of their own lives. They have emerged as whole persons, secure in the knowledge that they can take care of themselves and eminently capable of one day creating in their worlds the kind of satisfaction that comes from love-need fulfillment.

9

The joy of knowing another's world

Most of us find it very difficult to get along with other people, day after day and year after year. We discover early that in order to be moderately happy, we have to stay on speaking terms with our families, our teachers, our classmates, our friends, and our neighbors. As we grow older, we come into contact with still more teachers, as well as employers, coworkers, and eventually marriage partners and children. Because humans are inherently social beings, we must learn along the way how to deal with other people. And for some reason, we seem to have the most trouble learning to deal with those we love and want to keep on loving—those to whom we have committed ourselves to "love and honor" for as long as we live. The old familiar lyric about always hurting the person you love most is still true today.

The less secure we are in terms of our ability to fulfill our human needs, the more we try to control, change, or manipulate our partner into being the way we think he or she should be. We correct, we advise, we nag, we "suggest"—all in the name of "helping" our spouse to better handle his or her life. What we are really doing, however, is implying (or saying outright) that our partner's perceptions, judgments, wants, and behaviors do not correspond with ours. If we are miserable in our marriage, we go even further and insist that our partner is "making" us miserable. "If only my husband/wife were more like me," we think, "I know we'd be happier together." We do our best to make our partner more like us. And, even worse, we expect someone we love to be grateful to us when we attempt to straighten him or her out!

Attempting to change another person is something we have no right to do. When we move in on others and try to take control of their lives, we are depriving them of the opportunity to responsibly control their own world. By "world," I mean the whole spectrum of human needs, wants, perceptions, and behaviors that make up what an individual is.

I want to control my own world, and so do you. I want to be free to compare what I perceive with what I want and bring the two into harmony so that my needs are met. I want to be free to evaluate what I am doing and determine whether my behaviors are helping me to achieve my goals. I want to be free to examine and evaluate all the options open to me and then decide on a plan for my own future. Every person alive wants these things, but few of us seem willing to let others have them, too. Instead of allowing others to control their own world, we keep telling them about ours. We describe our wants and perceptions as if they're the only ones that matter, and when someone dares to have wants and perceptions that differ from ours, we insist that we're right and they're wrong. We expect that others will want to conform to our world as soon as we've shown them the way.

Long ago, humankind was surprised—and annoyed—to discover that the earth was not the center of the universe. In terms of human relationships, the majority of us are still living in the dark ages. We persist in thinking that our own particular world is the hub around which the rest of the universe revolves.

To get along with others, we must learn to respect their worlds. We live in a democracy, where laws have been written to protect our right to the "pursuit of happiness"—the pursuit of the fulfillment of all our needs. We are allowed to exercise that right as long as we refrain from interfering with another's attempt to do the same. What happens when we don't? In extreme cases, we land in jail. In less extreme cases, we may land in a divorce court.

In trying to control others, we not only deprive them of the opportunity to manage their own lives but also of the chance to learn how. As a consultant to various businesses, I often teach managers and supervisors how to teach their employees the art of controlling for their own individual wants and needs. Simply giving orders robs the employee of the freedom to experience the process of self-evaluation and growth that is so necessary to thinking and working things out on his or her own. It also defeats what ought to be the primary purpose of good management: teaching employees how to control their own performance responsibly within the context of their jobs and the company culture. Few supervisors are able to be with their employees throughout the entire working day; for a company to run smoothly, each employee must be able to make responsible and informed decisions within his or her area.

Like it or not, we are all teachers. This is especially evident when we are parents. In some ways, raising children is like supervising employees. If our parenting consists of nothing more than telling our children what to do, we are robbing them of the chance to learn responsible decision-making. If, on the other hand, we allow them to look at their own world, evaluate their wants in light of their needs, and pass judgment on their own behaviors and perceptions, we are preparing them to function more capably on their own.

In a marriage, the need to respect another's world takes on special importance. If I had spent the past thirty-two years telling Hester what was wrong with her world and doing my best to convince her to conform to mine, I doubt that we would be together today. This type of behavior is counterproductive at best and fatal at worst. For persons to live together, they must be able to fulfill their needs collectively and in harmony. For our marriage to remain healthy and happy and strong, I must continually remind myself that Hester has a world of her own. I must not only respect her right to live in that world without interference from me; I must also encourage her to do so.

One of the hardest lessons to learn is that other people are different from us. Their worlds are different from ours. Their perceptions are different from ours. So are their interests, their likes and dislikes, their preferences, and their habits. They get excited about things that bore us, and vice versa. Even two persons who love each other deeply cannot expect to complement each other at every turn. I know, for example, that there are certain kinds of movies Hester likes and others she can't stand. If I decide one evening that I want to watch "The Wild Bunch" on our videorecorder, I can assume with reasonable certainty that Hester won't want to watch it with me. That movie simply isn't part of her world. It's very much a part of the worlds of our sons, especially Nelson and Thomas, so I might invite them to watch it with me. But if I want to watch television with Hester, I'll look through the local listing to find a program that fits into her world—such as an opera or a ballet.

What happens when two persons who are married discover that they disagree about something that affects their daily lives? For instance, it's important to Hester's world that our son Luke keep his room clean and his clothes put away. She has been after him for years to be neater. I would also like Luke to be a bit more conscientious, but I approach the problem differently. I think that the best way to handle it is to leave Luke alone until his room gets so messy that he can't find anything in it. At that point, he usually does something about it.

Hester's world and my world aren't the only ones operating here, of course; there is also Luke's world. To him, a clean room and unwrinkled clothes aren't that important. He's willing to admit, though, that our opinions are important. He recognizes that each member of the family is responsible for keeping up his or her own part of the house.

It's up to Hester and me to either bring our two worlds into harmony or come to some other type of arrangement. Since my attitude toward Luke's room is more laissez-faire than hers, I could start criticizing her by saying, "Hester, you're being foolish" or "There's no need to be so strict with Luke about this." If I did this, though, I would in essence be suggesting that my way is "better" than hers and she should change. I would be trying to control her.

What I have decided to do instead is to listen to whatever she says without *making a judgment about it.* The result is that I don't have to deal with the conflict between her perception and mine. I have every confidence that she and Luke will be able to resolve the difficulty without me. Just because Hester and I love each other doesn't mean that we have to agree on everything. On the contrary, our love gives us room to disagree without putting our relationship in jeopardy.

But what if Hester simply can't ignore Luke's messy room and he just doesn't respond? Neither criticism nor anger will work here. They will only make matters worse. Spending quality time alone together on a daily basis is the only thing I know that will increase the probability that Luke will let Hester into his own world. In other words Luke must be able to perceive Hester's want, accept it and be willing to do something to help her get what she wants—not what *he wants, what she wants.* Her anger or criticism would make this less likely to happen; her involvement with Luke makes it more likely to happen. However, there is just no guarantee. Luke may never change. In this case Hester must decide if a clean room is worth the price of weakening her relationship with her son. This is her choice, and however she chooses she will no doubt get what she wants.

Finally, what if two persons have a serious problem, one that absolutely must be solved if they are going to get along and stay together? Again, criticism, anger, and other control mechanisms are not the answer here since they only make matters worse. What might be necessary is an attempt, through a third party such as a counselor, to approach his world with what is in her world—in other words—a search for common ground for compromise. If neither one wants to resolve the issues, then separation is the only course.

* * *

I had met with Alice and Bart together only twice when she telephoned me. There was something she needed to discuss with me in private.

"You know that Bart has seen other women off and on for years," she said. "What you don't know is that he went to visit his latest lover the week before we started coming to you. I honestly don't know what to do. What if he keeps wanting me *and* his lover? I don't think I can handle that."

"Does he know you know?" I asked.

"Not yet. In the meantime, what should I do?"

"Well," I began, "one alternative is to keep on working at your relationship with him. As the two of you get closer, he may not need or want other women anymore."

"I don't know if I can keep working at it," Alice admitted. "We already went through one separation, and it looks as if we're headed for another. I can't stand the thought of getting close to him again if that's how we're going to end up."

Since Alice was reluctant to work on her marriage, the only other choice she seemed to have was letting it go and getting a divorce. But she wasn't happy with that idea, either. There was one other option I asked her to consider: a discussion with Bart in which she would tell him everything she knew about his affair. She agreed.

We developed a plan of action for the discussion. She would begin by picking a time when both she and Bart were relaxed and fairly calm, and a place where they could talk without drawing others into their conflict or being interrupted.

We then discussed the best way for her to go about entering Bart's world with what she knew. We decided that she should begin by telling him what was in her own world. Specifically, she would describe to him what she wanted (a loving marriage); what she perceived (him as the person she wanted to love); and what she was attempting to do (spend more time with him and get their marriage back on the track).

When the three of us met again, we reviewed what had occurred during their discussion.

"I started off by telling Bart that I wanted to stay married to him and why," Alice began. "Then I told him how hard it was not to know what he wanted. Finally, I told him that I knew he had been seeing this other woman."

"I was surprised," Bart confessed. "But I guess it needed to come out."

"Then what happened?" I asked Alice.

"I told him I wanted to work at loving him, but not if he kept on seeing other women at the same time. I made it clear that I just couldn't deal with that."

When all the facts were out in the open, Alice and Bart could then honestly assess what their marriage meant to each of them and make an informed choice as to what they wanted to do next. Bart agreed to stop seeing other women and give his marriage a chance. Alice expressed her willingness to get close to him again. Having committed themselves to working on their marriage, the two of them could start making some real progress.

*   *   *

Unfortunately, honest discussions don't always have the desired result. Sometimes the person who is being confronted couldn't care less. The situations I find hardest and most painful to deal with are those in which one spouse is desperately trying to rebuild the marriage while the other is indifferent to his or her partner's efforts and struggles. Although this may sound simplistic, I believe that *most* couples could be very happy together if they were only willing to work harder at their relationship.

Interestingly, those couples who do put forth the most effort generally end up the happiest—*regardless of whether they stay married*. Even if two persons eventually decide to separate and divorce, the process of trying to solve their problems responsibly makes both of them stronger and more in control of their lives.

Calm discussions aren't always the easiest route to take. When two persons are furious with each other, it's better if they set their concerns aside and deal with them later, when they have calmed down somewhat. Whenever we're angry, our negative perceptions tend to outweigh our positive ones, and our behaviors are more erratic. We say things we don't mean and mean things we don't say.

For couples who have formed the habit of fighting or getting angry with each other, I recommend that they leave each other's presence temporarily and spend time alone doing something enjoyable. I suggest things like going for a walk, lifting weights at a local spa, running, washing the car, doing yoga, or exercising strenuously—anything that will get a person's perceptions onto something positive. If the activity benefits the person, so much the better. When we change our behavior, we can't help but change our perceptions. We can face whatever is bothering us later from a more rational, calm, positive perception of the world.

Talking about problems is seldom the way to solve them. Fantasy perceptions can easily be built through talking. Also, people often use a conversation as an excuse to air their feelings. Somewhere along the line, we've accepted the idea that our feelings "cause" us to be the way we are, and that if we verbalize them we can change them or make them go away. Getting our feelings "out," we believe, will free us from them. If we can't manage to do this ourselves, we turn for relief to the knights in shining armor—the drug industry—and take one medicine after another to soothe our out-of-control emotions, heal our troubles, and restore order to our disorganized lives. As a culture, we agree with the theory that people whose feelings run rampant are "emotionally disturbed" and can be "cured" by a variety of exotic medications. Drugs do nothing but reduce the pain of unresolved conflict; they cannot begin to help us learn responsible behaviors to more adequately fulfill our needs.

Another reason why even long, calm discussions do not always bear fruit is that in talking about feelings, we are often handicapped by a prevailing misconception of what feelings *are*. Too often, we confuse feelings with *perceptions*. When we ask someone to "tell us how you feel about what you just saw," we could easily—and more accurately—translate this into "tell us what you just perceived." Similarly, asking someone "How do you feel about this?" translates into "What do you *think* about this?" or even "What do you want?" The word "feeling" has become less and less precise.

It's when we blame our feelings as being the cause of our behaviors that we miss the point entirely. Claiming "I was too upset to work today," or "I felt so angry with my daughter that I couldn't help giving her a whack," or "I saw red, and the next thing I knew I was screaming at my husband" *gives us permission in our own minds to relinquish the responsibility for our actions.* By the same token, we commonly assume that "emotionally disturbed" people can't control themselves because their feelings have taken control of them. And this is simply not true.

Our feelings do not cause our actions; rather, they are *caused by* our actions. They are part of our behavioral system and a direct result of the things we choose to do and think. When I go running, for instance, my brain releases certain chemicals that react to what I am doing and cause me to feel how I am feeling. In that way, I know whether my needs—to get exercise, to control my body, to spend some time alone, to achieve a particular goal—are being met. If I am acting responsibly and fulfilling my needs, I will *feel* satisfied. In fact, *feelings are what we strive to produce to verify that we are doing or thinking something helpful.* But they should never be held up as an excuse for refusing to take responsibility for what we do and think, and they shouldn't be equated with our perceptions.

It's also possible to mistake one feeling for another. It's easy to fool ourselves into believing that the euphoria we feel after a sexual encounter is the feeling of love-need satisfaction, or that the sense of victory we have after winning an argument is an indication that our control-need has been fulfilled. But neither of these readings is accurate. We learn this soon enough as our "high" fades and reveals the true condition of our need-fulfillment: of emptiness and frustration after a meaningless sexual encounter or embarrassment and shame after a needless altercation. Ultimately, our feelings do tell us whether what we're doing and thinking is helping us. But they only mirror the effects of our actions and behaviors; they don't determine them.

Since feelings are a part of the behavioral system, they can be the consequence of perceptions—just as doing and thinking behaviors can. If, for example, we keep resurrecting certain negative perceptions from out of our past, these will be followed by negative feelings. A negative perception from the past could have to do with something we did, or someone else; it's the perception that's the issue, not the perpetrator.

Bringing up old negative perceptions again and again is one way to avoid dealing with the present. If we persist in recalling them, this can seriously impede any progress we're trying to make in the present. It is hard to change our perception of ourself or the world when we continually reinforce it. Often, however, this problem takes care of itself.

I once counseled a man whose wife had had an affair. He was having a hard time forgetting this, although he knew that he couldn't do anything about it—no human being has ever figured out a way to go back and change the past. He was eager to talk about the terrible thing his wife had done and how badly she had "hurt" his feelings, but I wouldn't allow him to. I didn't even admonish him to forget about the incident. Instead, I ignored it entirely and insisted that he focus on the way their marriage was now. We talked about specific things he could do to make it better, and specific things he was already doing that were having positive effects.

I took this approach because of something I had discovered long ago: namely, *the more we are able to satisfy our human needs in the present, the more readily past events are forgotten or relegated to a position of no importance.* It is only when we fail to meet our needs in the present that negative events in the past continue to haunt us and dominate our thoughts. And talking about past events only continues the painful memories and serves to use the negative past as an excuse for irresponsible behavior in the present. It is like trying to rid a cup of the air inside it by blowing into it. Pouring water into a cup gets rid of the air, and fulfilling our needs in the present relegates past negative events to only a memory.

As my client grew closer to his wife and as the two of them worked to strengthen their marriage by spending quality time alone together, his negative perception of his wife and what she had done began to change. He thought about her affair less frequently, and he began to change his feelings about the event in response to the new perceptions he was forming. He hadn't changed what had happened; he had only changed the one thing he had control over—his own perception of his wife.

Spending quality time alone with our partner is essential to maintaining a continual positive perception of him or her. The more satisfying that time together is, the stronger our positive perception becomes. When negative perceptions do creep in, we are better equipped to filter them out, ignore them, or turn them into positive perceptions rather than letting them drag us down. We revert to negative perceptions less often. The more programmed a perception becomes, the more difficult it is to alter it; spending quality time alone together on a daily basis is what locks in the positive perception of our partner that is so necessary to our getting along with him or her.

However, getting along means more than just quality time together and respecting another's world. *It also means making the effort to enter that world.* If we don't do this on a regular basis, then we have a roommate, not a marriage partner. For two persons to love each other, they must be able to pass freely and frequently in and out of each other's world, and without discord.

Having a strong positive perception of someone we love also makes it easier to move back and forth between his or her world and ours. When we respect our partner's world, we are in essence respecting the person who defines and owns that world. We are more likely to listen to what our spouse has to say, appreciate the things he or she does, and resist the temptation to take total control of the relationship.

Keeping the path open between your world and your spouse's enables you to talk about your problems with a far greater chance of success—especially if you have taken the time to calm down beforehand. In the context of a close, loving, committed, strong relationship, talking can be eminently useful. Before recommending it to couples I counsel, however, I make sure that their marriage is strong enough to sustain it through the continual practice of quality alone time activities. In a marriage that is already teetering on the brink of disaster, talking can be very dangerous.

Along with quality time, the secret of having a meaningful and useful dialogue lies in how willing and able you are to enter your partner's world without trying to rearrange it. Let's say, for instance, that you and your spouse are having money troubles. Your part of the conversation might go as follows: "Honey, do you want to work with me on this money problem we're having?"

This question puts you squarely in your spouse's world, specifically in the region of his or her wants. You are not beginning by saying what *you* think or want, or even what you think he or she should want; rather, you are entering his or her world with your hands raised in a gesture of peace and friendship.

If your spouse is also willing to talk, you can proceed. If not, you will have to wait. What if your partner never expresses the desire to work things out? Then your relationship is in serious trouble, since you can't force him or her to change. Remember, *you cannot enter another's world unless that person wants you there.* Forcing your thoughts on others is like pushing them—they will push back. Assuming that your spouse is open to cooperating with you on this particular problem, your next question might be: "Would you mind going over with me those areas where you see our agreements, and those where you see our differences?"

With this, you're remaining in your partner's world, but you're moving from the region of wants into the region of perceptions. Again, you're not listing *your* perceptions; you're asking him or her to take the floor.

What if your spouse wants to change the course of the discussion at this point—by delving into the past, bringing up old perceptions and hurts, or attempting to make you feel guilty? Don't get caught. Gently try to lead him or her back into the present by saying something like, "Honey, I can't undo the past. All I can do is talk with you about what we can do together now. The only way I'll know what to do is by finding out where we agree and where we differ."

At no time should you fall into the trap of criticizing or correcting your spouse. Make no judgments about what he or she is saying; simply perceive his or her comments as words that are neither good nor bad. Avoid the temptation to manipulate or control your partner; he or she will perceive this instantly, will perceive him- or herself as insecure and threatened by it, and attempt to get back at you by controlling you. Before you know it, you'll be in the middle of a power struggle, which is no place to be when you want to resolve a conflict calmly and reasonably.

Another reason for making no judgments about what your spouse is saying is that it keeps you from forming negative perceptions of him or her. If you do form these perceptions, you then have to deal with them in your own world, and to do this you must first leave his or her world behind.

Once you have gotten over this snag in your conversation, you should then try to find out what your spouse thinks should be done about the problem. You might ask: "How can we work things out in a way that's fair to both of us?"

Now you have entered the region of behaviors. As your partner replies, you should continue to refrain from passing judgment on what he or she is saying. You should respond to his or her suggestions by saying things like "I see" or "I understand," and when you need additional information, you should ask for it in a dispassionate tone. "Would you please explain a little further what you mean?" keeps the dialogue going, while "You aren't making yourself clear" or "You're confusing me" may slam the door—especially if your partner perceives comments of this type as threatening and controlling. Positioning yourself as the person with the problem—"I'm confused; can you help me out?"—is much more constructive than leveling accusations at your spouse.

If you get this far in your dialogue, you are well on your way to formulating a plan (a new behavior) that both you and your spouse can live and work with. If you take this approach to problem-solving whenever the need arises, you will eventually learn what your world has in common with your partner's. In return, he or she will become less reluctant to learn about your world. And this is what talking should accomplish—not the airing of dirty laundry. Reconciliation becomes easier when a relationship contains three ingredients: the ability to dialogue, programmed positive perceptions of each other, and quality time spent alone together.

Entering the world of someone you love involves more than just discussing problems, however. It requires a willingness on your part to find out what things are important to him or her and what he or she likes and dislikes. It means accepting the whole package that the other person is—complete with unique tastes, quirks, and foibles. Sometimes it means shutting your eyes to colors that clash or closing your ears to music you consider discordant or boring. When you criticize the way someone dresses or drives or sets the table or laughs, when you sneer at a novel someone is reading or scoff at a work of art that pleases him or her, you are stepping on a tender and exposed part of that person's own world.

It's equally damaging to ignore those attempts your partner makes to draw you into his or her world. Hester loves to talk about the people who come into her shop during the day; for me to refuse to listen would be cruel. I may not be dying to know everything she wants to tell me, and I may not be all that interested in her descriptions, but I force myself to hear her out for both our sakes. And I don't consider this at all hypocritical. She does the same for me, and we both find it eminently satisfying.

One of the greatest joys of getting to know others well lies in gaining admittance to their worlds. Our own worlds are limited to what we know, like, want, perceive, and do. As we seek to learn about the worlds of others, we open ourselves up to unlimited variety. It is exciting to find out what excites another person. It is fascinating to hear about someone else's experiences, to be exposed to opinions that differ from ours, to be in the presence of another thinking, observing, creating human being. To me, meeting someone for the first time is like going on a treasure hunt. What wonderful worlds we can find in others!

I am convinced that if people had this kind of interest in others, we would all be happier. Fewer people would spend their later years alone and lonely. The whole fabric of our society would become so much more complex and colorful, and the alienation so many of us experience would be replaced by a sense of belonging and community.

The ability to enter the worlds of those around us is not something we're born with. It's something we learn from others and should impart to others by serving as examples and by active teaching. One technique I have used with some of my clients and found successful is role playing. If, for example, I am counseling a woman who perceives her mother as cold and uncompromising, I might suggest that we try a little role play in an attempt to discover ways in which she might deal more effectively with her mother. "I'll be you, and you be your mother," I'll say. "Now let's have a conversation." More often than not, my client emerges from this experience with a better understanding of her mother's wants, needs, and perceptions. She may begin to perceive her mother in a whole new light. And she may discover in herself the willingness to take on more responsibility for the parent-child relationship.

The more often we enter the world of someone we love, the less self-centered we become and the more fully our needs are satisfied. We grow closer to that person. We learn to reconcile our differences and resolve our problems in nonthreatening, nonjudgmental, nondestructive ways. We learn what it means to be in love and to stay in love—an experience that can change us forever.

Again and again, I have watched couples lock into each other's worlds. Almost before they realize what is happening, they begin to perceive each other more positively. They find themselves wanting to do more things together, share more of themselves, and explore every facet of each other. One couple expressed this beautifully when they said: "We really didn't understand what you were talking about at first. Then we tried some of the things you suggested, and we began experiencing a closeness we had never even known existed. Not the physical closeness that's found in sex, but the closeness that comes from doing simple things alone together. Once we had that, we began to realize how little we knew about love and about each other. And we want to spend our lifetime learning."

Afterword

Beyond human needs

Our hearts are restless until they rest in Thee, O Lord. . . .
                                                   —St. Augustine

Throughout all of our lives, we are driven by the urge
to satisfy our basic and human needs. We feed our hunger and slake our thirst, seek out the company of others,
pursue activities that please and sustain us, have and
nurture children, gain some control over how and what
we do, love and are loved in return. Most of us, however, believe we are driven by still another urge: the
desire to move toward something that goes far beyond
our existence on this earth, to know our Maker and
return in some small measure the love so generously
bestowed upon us.

I believe that the human needs that motivate us are
our Maker's unique creative signature. These needs have
been designed to lead us toward the Designer. But we
are also a self-directing species: Whether and how we
choose to satisfy our needs is up to us. It is significant
that when we try to fulfill them at the expense of others,
we are left feeling frustrated and empty.

The love-need is certainly the most difficult to satisfy.
It also holds the promise of yielding the most rewards.
The more completely our love-need is met, the happier
we are and the closer we draw toward the Creator of
this need. And the more we learn to love others, the
more incumbent it becomes on us to teach them what
we have learned, to pass along the knowledge our experiences have revealed to us. Perhaps this book will
lead you to a clearer understanding of your own love-
need and how you can work to fulfill it; perhaps it will
lead you one step nearer to the Author of love itself.